A PRACTICAL GUIDE TO BUSINESS PROCESS RE-ENGINEERING

A PRACTICAL GUIDE TO BUSINESS PROCESS RE-ENGINEERING

Mike Robson and Philip Ullah

Gower

© Mike Robson 1996

All rights reserved. No part of this publication may be reproduced, stored in a retrieval system, or transmitted in any form or by any means, electronic, mechanical, photocopying, recording or otherwise without the permission of the publisher.

Published by
Gower Publishing Limited
Gower House
Croft Road
Aldershot
Hampshire GU11 3HR
England

Gower
Old Post Road
Brookfield
Vermont 05036
USA

Mike Robson has asserted his right under the Copyright, Designs and Patents Act 1988 to be identified as the author of this work.

British Library Cataloguing in Publication Data

Robson, Mike, 1944–
   A practical guide to business process re-engineering
   1. Reengineering (Management) 2. Organizational change
   I. Title II. Ullah, Philip
   658.4'06

ISBN 0–566–07577–6

Library of Congress Cataloging-in-Publication Data

Robson, Mike.
   A practical guide to business process re-engineering /
   Mike Robson and Philip Ullah.
     p.   cm.
   Includes bibliographical references and index.
   ISBN 0–566–07577–6 (hardcover)
   1. Reengineering (Management).   I. Ullah, Philip.   II. Title.
HD58.87.R63 ·1996   95–40204
658.4'063—dc20   CIP

Typeset in Palatino by Raven Typesetters, Chester and printed in Great Britain by Biddles Ltd. Guildford.

Contents

List of Figures		vii
Preface		ix
1	An Introduction to Business Process Re-engineering	1
2	Managing by Process	11
3	An Overview of Business Process Re-engineering	27
4	Requirements for Success	37
5	Roles and Resources	45
6	Structuring Business Process Re-engineering	61
7	Understanding the Process	75
8	Mapping the Process	87
9	Tools	105
10	Principles	121
11	Managing the Change	145
Further Reading		155
Index		157

List of Figures

2.1	Process inputs and outputs	16
6.1	Prioritizing processes	71
8.1	Process environment diagram	89
8.2	Original process environment diagram	90
8.3	Data flow diagram	92
8.4	Second-level data flow diagram	93
8.5	Process dictionary	95
8.6	Input/output consistency	96
8.7	Recommended symbols for use on flow charts	98
8.8	Flow chart for job repair process	100
8.9	Data flow diagram for job repair process	101
9.1	Nine-dot problem	108
9.2	Solution to the nine-dot problem	108
10.1	PC purchasing process	124
10.2	Re-engineered PC installation process	126
10.3	Sales lead handling process	128
10.4	Changing role of suppliers in the purchasing process	131
10.5	Installing a Local Area Network (LAN)	133

Preface

Business Process Re-engineering (BPR) has been hailed by some as the 'latest and greatest' in a long line of management initiatives, as something that makes all other previous improvement processes redundant. BPR is sometimes talked about as a replacement for concepts such as Total Quality. It is nothing of the kind and senior executives should understand this before they rush off, re-engineer everything in sight and in the process destroy much that is valuable. In fact a considerable number have already done this and that number will undoubtedly grow, as it has done for every 'new' management initiative that has ever been developed. Please don't add to it; it's very painful and, in the long run, self-defeating.

It is surely much better to understand what BPR involves, to think carefully about its potential use in your particular organization, to see how it should fit within the framework of a company-wide improvement process, and then to plan and execute it in a thorough and professional manner.

This book explains how to gain the most from what is, potentially, an extraordinarily useful and powerful tool; an emphasis on 'how to do it successfully' rather than 'what is it all about?' distinguishes this book from others that have been written on the subject.

BPR is not new, at least in a conceptual sense. What it does is to use advances in technology, not just computer technology but also the technologies of managing change and managing people, to enable us to be much more radical in the way we run our organizations than has been possible in the past. This is its newness and its excitement. To make it work, however, as with everything else, it has to be done with knowledge, skill and care.

Do it, but do it properly, because BPR is worth doing properly.

Mike Robson
Philip Ullah

1 An Introduction to Business Process Re-engineering

In a world where change is the only constant there is a need for tools and techniques to help organizations become more effective. In a competitive world there is a need for ways to stay ahead of the field or to catch up before it is too late. In a complex world there is a need for mechanisms that can make apparently complicated things simpler.

Business Process Re-engineering (BPR) is an undeniably powerful tool that can help in all of these circumstances, which is why it has created such interest in organizational circles even though it is still, relatively speaking, in its infancy as a management technique.

It is becoming more difficult to deny that continuous improvement in all its forms is a vital philosophy for any organization today if it wishes to survive and succeed in the medium let alone the long term. In fact it is probably a truism. It is also relevant to note that the changing nature of the world around us has created this situation and that change is not happening at a steady linear rate but is increasing exponentially.

As consultants whose jobs entail making periodic visits to clients we recollect that it is not that many years ago that it was possible to revisit organizations and restart from where they were a month or even two months later. It is entirely different today. Harold Wilson, the British Prime Minister in the 1960s, once said, 'a week is a long time in politics'. A week is a long time in many of our organizations nowadays; the structure changes, someone gets promoted or sacked, a competitor does something either very clever or very silly that demands an immediate response, and so it goes on. Those who are at the beginning of their career will remember only these circumstances, which is fine as long as they, and all of us, also remember that in a changing world standing still actually means going backwards, and blindly protecting the *status quo* is probably the most dangerous stance of all.

In these circumstances it is sometimes not possible to keep up purely by a process of continually finding small-scale improvements to the processes that currently exist. Processes can become obsolete in the same way as can products, often with frightening regularity, and if this happens there is no point in trying to fix or to improve them; better to start again from the beginning and create something new that fits the new situation.

BPR is a tool that is designed specifically to help in circumstances where large-scale improvements are needed that cannot be brought about within the existing format of the processes currently being used. This does not mean that BPR replaces continuous improvement, far from it. Once a process has been re-engineered, which is a project, it will need the techniques of continuous improvement, which is a process, to be applied to it if it is to avoid decay.

ORIGINS OF BPR

The origins of BPR are generally recognized as being in two articles, written in 1990 by Hammer[1] and Davenport and Short,[2] and no one would want to deny them the contribution that they have made. However, though the term BPR is only a few years old, many of the underlying concepts that it is based on are much older.

For decades managers have been taught the difference as Drucker defined it between efficiency and effectiveness. Efficiency is 'doing things right' whereas effectiveness is 'doing the right things'. It has been pointed out that we often tend to concentrate on becoming more and more efficient, not realizing that we spend much of our time doing the wrong things. So organizations are full of people who spend a large proportion of their working lives producing outputs that are accurate, on time, well presented and so on; but unfortunately are neither necessary nor used by the people for whom they were produced.

During the 1980s Total Quality was introduced into many organizations. The important subject of the links between this process and BPR are dealt with later in this chapter, but it was this concept that introduced us to the idea of process management. Many of the techniques of Total Quality stress the need to look anew at the work we do, and for what purpose we do it, and they provide us with valuable knowledge for Business Process Management (BPM). Techniques such as Method for Analysing Processes (MAP), In-Department Evaluation of Activity (IDEA), Process Perception Analysis (PPA) have been used for ten years or more, as has Process Quality Management (PQM) which is described in detail in Chapter 6 since it plays an important part in any comprehensive Business Process Re-engineering project.

> There is much that can be done to achieve Excellence by 'putting our own house in order', of this there is no doubt. Equally there are many problems, issues and opportunities that can be, and all too often are, overlooked if this is the sole focus. It is often

staggering to find the extent of the simplification of work processes which is possible when they are looked at in an organised way. Jobs become embedded within processes which at the time seemed, and maybe were, logical and useful, but for whatever reasons are now not needed for the fulfilment of the requirements of the next customer who receives the output.[3]

What BPR gives us, when it is applied well, is a means of achieving the scale of gains that it has long been recognized were available. Historically, however, most organizations have had neither the technology nor the courage to exploit these opportunities. The interest that currently surrounds BPR stems mainly from the dramatic claims that are made for it as a way of achieving massive benefits and this is indeed a main purpose of the technique both from the point of view of better satisfying customers and also as a way of improving business performance.

WHY BOTHER WITH BPR?

There are a number of factors that can be significant in triggering an organization's BPR effort and increasingly the main one is what competitors have been able to achieve with the technique and the stimulus, or maybe just the fear, that this achievement has engendered. The second main trigger is the chief executive or senior director with a vision who sees the 'blue sky' opportunity offered by radical change and development.

Though in many ways the second route gives the best starting point, this route often has inherent difficulties as most people are not visionaries and so it can be hard to convince others of the wisdom of choosing BPR and risking a major upset of the equilibrium. In addition the feasibility of making gains of the scale envisaged is always questioned by many, and not just the sceptics.

On the other hand if a competitor has already started BPR and is claiming great benefits it is easier to make the case to the people in the organization that this is not a 'nice to do' add on to their normal work, rather that it is required for their very survival. It is by no means insignificant that analyses of organization-wide change processes indicate quite clearly that the most successful change processes are those that start from the background of threat. It is probably not too much of a generalization to say that the greater the threat the higher the chance of success as long as the perception of threat is genuine. The logic of this is that real threat focuses the mind, a required attribute if the true potential benefits are to be realized.

WHAT IS BPR?

At the outset we will do well to establish what BPR is and where it fits among the host of new initiatives that are available to management today. By doing this we will also clear up a number of dangerous misconceptions that have already begun to surround the subject.

First then, a definition: 'BPR is the creation of entirely new and more effective business processes, without regard for what has gone before.' BPR uses a variety of tools and techniques within an orderly structure and is primarily cross-functional in its focus, certainly at the macro-organizational level. This said, sub-processes are sometimes contained within one function or department and BPR can be applied to them as well.

There are a number of important consequences of this description. First it involves starting from a blank page, and in many ways, a blank mind or at least one that is clear and able to think outside the constraints of present systems, ways of thinking and assumptions. Most people are creatures of habit who come to view the way that things are done as being both normal and inevitable. To use BPR effectively we need to break this habit, although it is far from easy to do.

Second, BPR involves questioning assumptions. Our lives are governed by the assumptions we make about a whole variety of issues; it is the only way that we can cope with the huge mass of information that we are presented with. This applies in our private lives: for example, many people in the UK have for years assumed that they would be better off if they owned their own house; this was the natural order of things, as obvious as night following day – and for many years it was. But we live in a world of change, and today thousands of people are caught in a negative equity trap that had seemed impossible, and now seems impossible to escape from.

Similarly in our organizations. For years it was assumed that errors were inevitable and so a certain amount of leeway we needed to accommodate this. In manufacturing industry AQLs (Acceptable Quality Levels) would be set at 95 per cent, allowing for a 5 per cent failure rate, and this was viewed as sophistication! Most other functions just accepted that 'you can't win them all' and didn't even bother to set standards, they just tried to fix things when they went wrong. Then it all changed, as this widely quoted article from the Toronto *Sun* newspaper demonstrates:

> IBM, the computer giant decided to have some parts made in Japan and in the specification they set an Acceptable Quality Level of 3 defective parts per 10,000 for the job. When they took delivery there was an accompanying letter which said,

Dear Sirs,

We Japanese have hard time understanding North American business practices. But the three defective parts per 10,000 have been included and are wrapped separately. Hope this pleases.
Yours sincerely.

This is not to say that we should never make assumptions because, frankly, we have to if we are to retain any semblance of sanity. However, when undertaking a BPR project there is no place for prior assumptions about what should or should not be, or what is normal and inevitable. This again is a key feature of the technique, nothing is sacrosanct.

The third consequence of the definition of BPR is that it requires a considerable amount of creativity, which is the linking together of objects and ideas that were previously unrelated. Many of the great leaps forward in science have been creative intuitions that were only later proved mathematically, Einstein's Theory of Relativity and Crick and Watson's discovery of the structure of DNA being just two of many examples.

BPR depends on this kind of thinking. For example people have worked in offices since the start of the Industrial Revolution, the telephone was invented a hundred years ago, and modems some twenty years back. The use of personal computers began to spread in the 1970s and they have been in common use for the last ten years. Offices are expensive to own or rent. Many people spend huge amounts of time travelling to work, where they sit at a computer all day long. Their journey to work costs money, uses scarce resources and often pollutes the environment. 'But people have always worked in offices' was, and still is for many, the conventional wisdom. There are other options if only we allow them to permeate. Home-based working is now an accepted fact for many.

The fourth issue that stems from the definition concerns the use of technology. Some people have fallen into the trap of thinking that BPR involves the use of technology and nothing else. Such a view is far from the truth, and is very dangerous, in fact technology is to be seen simply as one of the enablers of radical change. This is not to play down the role of technology since it must be said that many of the existing opportunities depend on the technological advances that are now such a normal part of our lives. Furthermore if BPR is to last as an important tool it will have to continue to use new technology, as it is developed, to spearhead even more radically different, and more effective, ways of doing things.

In practice much of the business of re-engineering involves other elements, for example, the appropriate use of the principles of process management, a range of problem-solving activities, the application of organization development and Total Quality techniques, and up-to-date and effective ways of motivating, managing and leading people.

BPR should not be viewed fundamentally as an information technology (IT) driven strategy since this may well lead to inappropriate and costly decisions being made. Information technology is available, its potential should be understood at least conceptually by all those involved, not just IT experts, and it should be the servant of re-engineering, never its master. Professional expertise will be required from a range of sources if BPR is to fulfil its potential and IT experts should have their rightful place as part of the whole team, not necessarily as its leader or, indeed, as the driver of change.

Finally, BPR is concerned with replacing the current process with one that is much more effective for both the customer and the organization itself. From the customer's perspective shorter lead times and no bureaucracy, for example, will help to meet requirements faster and with no frustration. From the organization's perspective there will be less cost, more competitiveness, better service and so the opportunity to gain more market share.

WHERE DOES BPR FIT?

If this is a definition of what BPR is and some of the implications of the technique, the next question asks how it fits with other approaches. In answering this question we must recognize that BPR is a tool, one of many that are available for managers who are interested in improving the performance of their organization. It can help to achieve dramatic change and improvement, more so than most of the other mechanisms, but it remains a tool. BPR is organized on a project basis; it is not a concept, it is not a complete and coherent way of running an organization.

Some people attempt to position BPR as a replacement for Total Quality or in some way 'beyond Total Quality'. This is so far from the truth that it must call into question the knowledge and understanding, or integrity, of those who make such pronouncements and is worthy of a little further explanation. It is maybe unfortunate but none the less true that Western business society is notoriously short term in its thinking. We all know that the phenomenon exists, we understand the damage it does and as yet we have for the most part been unsuccessful in addressing the issue.

A number of effects stem from this thinking, including that there will always be money to be made out of creating the next popular 'flavour of the month' and pronouncing the previous one obsolete however much longer-term damage it does to the many gullible organizations that believe such stories.

There are also all too many managers who see their own careers being promoted by the tactical use of new management thinking for their own gain. A while ago we were talking to a senior manager in a large biscuit-making organization about the best way of making further progress. The organization is known for its forward-looking views. We began to talk about the opportunities that there were in the area of empowerment when he interrupted and said, 'No, that's no good, I'm looking for the next flavour of the month, not the last one!' We found it difficult to maintain the conversation after that.

The fact is that most of the innovations in management thinking over the years have made a lot of sense as a part of what we could call 'good management practice'. These innovations have failed in some organizations because they have been improperly understood and then introduced and managed badly, but they remain a part of 'good management practice' none the less. Far too many organizations in the West still have to get used to this idea and until they do we will fail to make the most of the philosophies and techniques that are available to us and the resources, both human and other, that we deploy.

For many years we have sought to persuade organizations that we have helped to introduce and sustain Total Quality that they must think of it as a process, an ongoing process of organization change and development. We have heard thousands of people talk about their 'Total Quality Programmes', and have pointed out that programmes have a beginning, a middle and an end. We have explained that the only way to sustain Total Quality is to make it the normal way that things are done in the organization, not just for a period of time but for ever. Total Quality when it is introduced with understanding, skill and care is genuinely a complete and coherent way of running an organization; if it is not it will invariably fail after a period of time.

Successful Total Quality processes use a wide variety of tools and techniques to assist with the aim of creating change and improvement. Some of them have been 'borrowed', others have been designed specifically to meet new requirements and challenges. New techniques to help organizations confront their problems and opportunities are being developed all the time and BPR must be seen as one of these rather than something that replaces the 'umbrella' concept.

If the organization already has a reasonably mature change process, for example one that has been worked on consistently over a period of five years or more, it should have a sound infrastructure in place and be using a range of tools and techniques as a normal part of the way that things are done. In these circumstances the addition of a new technique within the whole framework should present no particular difficulty.

Problems that would need managing could be caused if the underlying culture of the organization was likely to be seriously affected by the application of the new technique. If, for example, the implicit or explicit culture has been one of staff involvement in improvement within the norm of job security, BPR could well be seen to threaten this and disrupt the whole process unless it is managed with consummate skill and care.

On the other hand an organization that has no formal process and wants to begin using BPR should recognize that unless a sound infrastructure is developed the most likely result is a first flush of enthusiasm and apparent progress followed by a rapid decline and a project consigned to the, already crowded, scrap heap of management gimmicks.

The infrastructure that is needed includes the various dimensions of organizational culture that are part of the best formed change processes. These invariably include, for example, a set of behavioural standards and a clearly defined mission. These statements are designed to be understandable, communicable, believable and usable throughout the organization, and are used routinely by people at all levels. The infrastructure also demands a continuous concern to develop the 'health' of the organization in such things as its structure, the way that it is managed, the communication process, the level of genuine customer orientation to both internal as well as external customers and, finally, the extent of 'psychological ownership' that exists among different levels of staff.

There has never been a successful whole change process that has relied entirely on one tool or technique, and it is highly unlikely that there ever will be. Frankly the world always has been too complex for that, and now, of course it is far more so. Organizations that do not have an established change process in place, and who want to use BPR, will do well to recognize that they will require other techniques to do the parts of the job that BPR is not equipped for and does not pretend to offer. They should also recognize that it is always better to have access to a holistic model when considering the entire process of change as it applies to their organization.

BPR is undeniably an effective process that is exciting and rewarding when handled well. This involves understanding the precise nature of the technique and what it demands in the way of new thinking. Also required is the ability to see where BPR fits within a total process of organizational change and development and careful, skilful management to avoid the many traps. If we have the courage to take them, enormous opportunities are available providing we use the tool wisely.

NOTES

1. Hammer, M. (1990), 'Reengineering work: don't automate, obliterate', *Harvard Business Review*, July–August, pp. 104–12.
2. Davenport, T.H. and Short, J.E. (1990), 'The new industrial engineering: information technology and business process redesign', *Sloan Management Review*, Summer, pp. 11–27.
3. Robson, M. (1986), *The Journey to Excellence*, p. 155, Wantage, Oxon: MRA International.

2 Managing by Process

In this chapter we will explain what business processes are, examine the idea of process management and explore how it differs from traditional functional management. We will also look at the potential benefits that can be derived from this new way of thinking.

Organizations, for the most part today, are structured in functions and hierarchies and most people have been brought up with the belief, not only that this is the most natural and efficient way of organizing, but that it is the only way of organizing. This has been the case ever since organizations began to be studied in a coherent way in the late nineteenth century.

Scientific Management, developed by F.W. Taylor, is probably the best known expression of this set of views. He reasoned that work could be performed most efficiently if it was broken down into simple elements and if people, especially operators, were deployed by management as specialists, concentrating on one simple part of the job. He also believed firmly in the importance of the role of management. 'It is only through enforced standardization of methods, enforced adoption of the best implements and working conditions, and enforced cooperation that this faster work can be assured. And the duty of enforcing the adoption of standards and enforcing this cooperation rests with the management alone.'[1] The natural conclusion of these views was to promote organization structures that were specialized into functions.

Taylor was not the only one of the early management thinkers to come to this view. Henri Fayol has been called the 'father' of management theory even though he is not as well known as Taylor. He believed that management was the subject of universal principles that, once isolated, could be taught. He developed a list of 14 principles, the first of which concerned the division of work and stated, 'The principle of specialization of labour in order to concentrate activities for more efficiency'.

Functional specialization was also a central tenet for Max Weber, the originator of the word and the theory of 'bureaucracy'. He believed that bureaucracy was the most efficient way of managing complex organizations and claimed that it was superior to any other approach in precision, stability, the stringency of its discipline, and its reliability. Weber believed that there were six 'building blocks' of bureaucracy, the first of which was functional specialization.

Though the ideas of these pioneers of management theory are largely discredited by today's thinkers, they still have an enormous influence on organizations all over the world. Certainly the vast majority are structured around the idea of functions and organized on the basis of specialists performing specialist tasks. So deeply entrenched is the conventional wisdom of this approach that it is only recently that anyone even thought about it, let alone asked questions or provided alternative possibilities.

THE PROBLEMS OF FUNCTIONAL MANAGEMENT

Though functional management is so widely used, it has been recognized for many years that it gives rise to a number of difficulties. Different functions often take a very parochial view, and are uninterested in issues that do not appear to affect them directly. It is common, for example, to find accounts departments that are interested only in the production of the management and financial information and are totally unconcerned about the factors that make the situation what it is. People often seem to behave as if there is actually no link between the two.

Another common feature of functional organizations is that destructive competition between functions seems often to be pursued more vigorously than competition with outside competitors. The classic example of this is probably the age old conflict between sales and marketing on the one hand and manufacturing on the other. It is not only the endless finger-pointing that takes place in meetings and the countless memos and reports which seem designed solely to expose the stupidity of the other party, it is also the untold informal discussions that take place between salespeople, among marketeers and between production personnel again concentrating entirely on the difficulties that the other department is causing them. If one tenth of all this energy, brainpower and time went into finding ways of beating the competition surely something beneficial would come out of it.

Communication is also often massively slowed down by over-strict adherence to the bureaucratic requirement to pass messages up the line to the head of the function before they can be passed across and then down the line in another function, rather than directly to the intended recipient. This happens for a number of reasons, primarily that there is insufficient trust in the motives of people in the other functions and therefore a fear of being caught out or trapped in some way.

Take an incident that happened only a couple of weeks ago. The small management team of a production facility on a fairly remote Scottish island which we have been asked to equip to be capable of operating as an autonomous work group, contacted the IT, Accounts and Sales departments on the mainland to request that some information be sent to them routinely, and that it would make sense for the member of the Sales force responsible for the products that they made to visit them periodically. They sent a copy of their note to the Managing Director. It all sounds, and was, very simple and straightforward, until, that is, the Production Director got to hear of it! They were never to contact anyone without it going through him; they were certainly never to get in touch with the Managing Director, despite his direct invitation to do so, and so on. An absurd amount of precious time was wasted.

The other issue with communication in a functional environment is that sometimes it simply does not exist, sometimes people seem to go about the business of their own function or department oblivious to all of the activity around them, which should be of profound interest and concern. It is no wonder that so many organizational problems are of a cross-functional nature. Yet the functional approach has endured because until recently there were perceived to be no alternatives.

BUSINESS PROCESSES

Although people involved in production have thought in terms of manufacturing processes for decades, it is less than twenty years ago that the idea of business processes was first mooted, and was greeted, for the most part, with complete indifference. Even the few that expressed any interest at all were largely sceptical that the idea had any real merit and it was only with the widespread application of Total Quality in organizations, that the idea of Business Process Management began to gain currency.

It was recognized, somewhat slowly and painfully, that organizations spend enormous amounts of time and money managing the functional hierarchy. For most managers this is the sole purpose of their working lives. Yet work does not go up and down functional hierarchies, it flows across the organization in a series of business processes that are, in most organizations, owned and managed by no one!

Let us consider for a moment what 'work' actually goes up and down the 'ladder'. One main activity is authorization; a subordinate takes a piece of work to the boss for permission to proceed with a particular course of action. Another is decision-making which, as we know, can be handled in a whole variety of different ways but which results in the 'boss' either accepting or rejecting a proposition and, generally speaking, sending the subordinate off to take action on the decision. A third such activity is direct instruction from the senior to the junior to do a certain piece of work or to take a certain course of action.

Now let us look at work laterally rather than hierarchically: an operator in the production area collects details of all of the overtime that has been worked that week and passes it to a clerk in the accounts department for processing; the sales office staff gather orders for the forthcoming period from the sales force, collate them and pass them on to the production planning department for scheduling; the engineers fill out a requisition form for new parts and pass it to purchasing for action, and so on.

Reflect on these examples. Where is the activity taking place which really adds value to the task of achieving the fundamental goals of the organization? It is, of course, a rhetorical question. But it does not stop there, we can go even further by posing the question that if we were organizing the work from scratch, who would perform the activities in the hierarchical list.

The first activity was authorization. Look around many organizations and you cannot fail to be surprised at the low level at which authorization is deemed necessary. Sometimes the value of the request must be lower than the value of the time that it takes for the manager to write the word 'authorized' and then to sign it!

The second set of activities were to do with decision-making. If the decisions refer to the normal course of the work of the subordinate, which they often do, a legitimate question is, who is in the best position to judge the appropriate course of action? Bringing someone else into the equation who, however senior, does not know the intricacies of the situation, will usually serve to confuse the issue and will often actually raise rather than lower the chances of an inappropriate decision being made!

Third were the occasions when the hierarchy gives direct instructions to do work, and again by observation of many different organizations there are many circumstances where this appears to be rather superfluous since the people concerned already know what they have to do and are perfectly willing and able to get themselves organized and go ahead and do it.

This may seem a rather harsh assessment of the role of functional management, and of course it only tells one side of the story. None the less there is enough validity in it for it to be of use in provoking the questioning of assumptions that previously were taken for granted.

So what is a business process? Quite simply it is a flow of work passing from one person to the next, and for larger processes probably from one department to the next. Processes can be defined at a number of levels but they will always have a defined beginning, a number of steps in the middle and a defined end. There is no standard list of processes and organizations should develop their own, not least because this discipline will facilitate a greater understanding of their own situation when viewed in process terms. It is remarkable the insights that so often emerge from working out the business processes of an organization even at a macro-level. Linkages and relationships that were ignored or not recognized are suddenly seen to be central to the effective functioning of the whole organization, let alone the particular process concerned.

For the sake of illustration, however, at the macro-level typical processes might include procurement, distribution, billing and accounts receivable. These may sound rather like functions but when defined as processes it is clear that they are not. For example, the billing process might start with the completion of an order form by a salesperson, and might go on to include production scheduling, confirmation of delivery from distribution, the generation of an invoice in financial accounts, credit control and banking. The process might end with the passing of information to management accounts. If this were the case then it is clear that a number of different functions are involved and this is a key characteristic of defining work in process terms.

A macro-level process can be broken down into sub-processes, for example ordering, distribution, credit control which are defined in more detail, but the principle is the same, that we are recording the flow of work as it passes from person to person. There are no hard and fast rules about how broadly or narrowly processes should be defined and organizations do come to different views even when they are dealing with processes that appear to be similar. In practice this does not matter as long as the processes specified represent coherent and whole flows of work and steps are not left out. This also applies when defining sub-processes which should be the natural breakdown of the bigger whole.

PROCESS BOUNDARIES

Processes are flows of work and they have boundaries, in other words beginnings and ends. For any one process these limits are determined by the initial or primary inputs that start it off, which are 'delivered' by its primary suppliers, and the output that occurs at the end which is for the

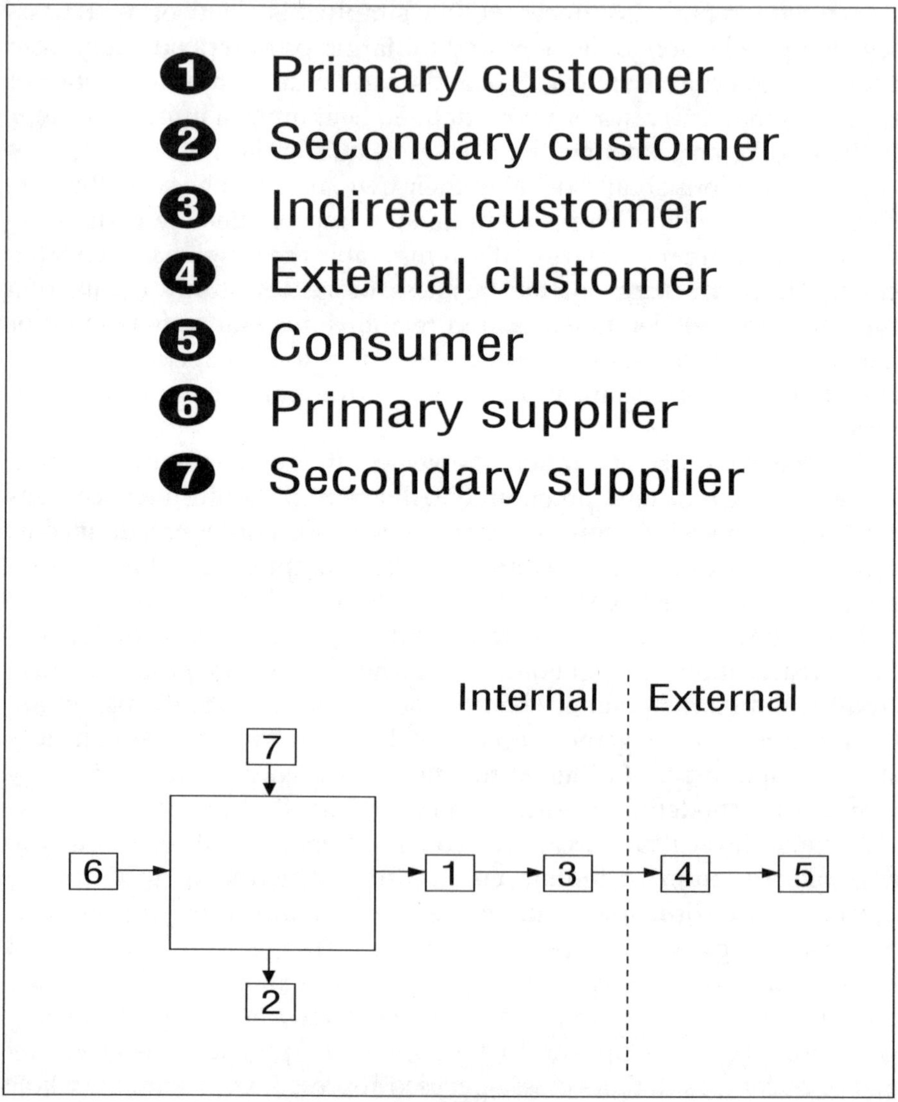

① **Primary customer**
② **Secondary customer**
③ **Indirect customer**
④ **External customer**
⑤ **Consumer**
⑥ **Primary supplier**
⑦ **Secondary supplier**

Internal | External

Figure 2.1   Process inputs and outputs

benefit of its primary customers. For example, the primary input to the billing process could be the receipt of confirmed orders in the sales office. The primary output of a process can be tangible, as in the purchase of a new piece of equipment, or intangible, such as the provision of certain information or a particular service. The primary output for the billing process mentioned above could be the banking of cheques.

Once the process has started there will be a number of secondary inputs that enter and are required to complete it. For example, management information provided by the IS department may be needed at various stages. When re-engineering a process how these secondary inputs are produced is no concern of the process under scrutiny and they are not subjected to analysis at the time. If they need to be worked on it should be through a different re-engineering project or using an alternative improvement technique.

In the same way that there are secondary inputs, there are invariably secondary outputs. These are produced as by-products of the process and are not the main purpose. An example here might be that a report on the amount of overtime worked by staff is produced as a part of a manufacturing process. Secondary outputs usually initiate other processes. In this example the overtime report could be a primary input into a remuneration process. These different inputs and outputs are summarized diagrammatically in Figure 2.1.

The only purpose of a process is to meet the requirements of its customers, of which there can be up to five different kinds in any process: first the primary customers who are those that receive the primary output; then there are secondary customers who are outside the process and receive the secondary outputs; third there are indirect customers who do not receive the primary output but are next along the line so they will be affected if the output is late or defective in any way. The fourth kind of customer is external, that is outside the company, and they receive the output of the process, so they could include distributors, agents, retailers, other organizations and so on. Finally there are consumers who are the indirect external customers, in other words you and me! There will not always be all of these categories and indeed there will be times when there is an overlap, for example a restaurant where the primary customer might be the same as the external customer and also the consumer.

CORE AND SUPPORT PROCESSES

In any organization there exist both core and support processes and it is necessary to understand the difference between them. The core processes are the operational processes of the business and result in the production of the outputs that are required by the external customer. The support processes are those that enable the primary process to exist. An example again might be a restaurant where the core process was the supply of quality food to the diner's table. Support processes here could include the table-clearing and washing-up process, the billing and accounts process and so on.

BENEFITS OF MANAGING PROCESSES

Potentially there are wide-ranging benefits to be gained from introducing a greater understanding of and orientation towards the management of business processes. For example, in these circumstances there should be a far more effective co-ordination of work as it flows from department to department with consequently fewer errors and a greater ability to meet the requirements of the customer right first time, on time, every time. Customer awareness should improve, usually dramatically, conflict between departments should be reduced as should delays between different steps in the process.

In functionally structured organizations what happens at the interfaces between departments often resembles border skirmishes in a long-running guerrilla war! Even where this is not the case and there is no particular antagonism there exist many opportunities for things to go wrong and therefore for customers to suffer a less than adequate service.

An example of this comes from a hospital and concerns the catering process. A customer (patient) survey had revealed that there was considerable dissatisfaction with the quality of the food that was being delivered to the bedside and so an investigation was set under way. The departments involved were first the ward medical staff who took the patients' food orders at the start of the process and also served the food at the end of it. Second was the kitchen whose people were concerned with the production of the food, and third were the porters whose job it was to deliver the trolleys containing the food to the wards.

The investigators talked to all concerned and, predictably, everyone said that it could not possibly be their fault! They established, however, that there was a laid down procedure governing the responsibilities of the different departments. An analysis of this revealed that the porters' responsibility ended at the door of the ward as they left the food outside for the nurses to collect, take inside and serve to the patients.

Observation of the process by the investigating team showed that the problem was that the trolleys were often left outside in the corridor for up to three hours before being collected by the nurses. Everyone was actually performing their part of the process perfectly well; the orders were accurate, the food was well prepared, the porters delivered it quickly and properly, the nurses served it to the patients; the problem was that no one was co-ordinating and managing the process as a whole, and the end result was an unmitigated disaster.

PROCESS MANAGEMENT IN PRACTICE

Many organizational problems are of a cross-functional nature so the next question to ask is how the idea of business processes can be applied in practice to help management to be more effective and to aid the improvement of performance. There are three possibilities that reflect different levels of concern, commitment and courage on the part of the organization; they are cross-functional problem-solving, defining and managing processes and introducing process structures.

CROSS-FUNCTIONAL PROBLEM-SOLVING

The first and simplest option is to use the idea of business processes to identify suitable subjects for problem-solving groups to work on and this can be done with different levels of formality. At its simplest, based on a broad and not too deep understanding of the idea of business processes, the senior team of an organization could have a discussion about all the flows of work and the cross-functional issues that are causing problems. Following on from this priorities can be established and cross-functional groups can be set up to tackle them. These groups will need to use an orderly process to guide them in their work and there is no reason to suppose that they cannot be successful and make a useful contribution to the improvement process.

There are now two alternative possibilities as far as methodology is concerned. The first is to use a conventional problem-solving structure to define the problem, analyse and collect data about it, develop and test the alternative possible solutions before coming to a preferred option. The second way of tackling the opportunity is to use a systematic Business Process Re-engineering approach.

The first of these, the conventional problem-solving group, is relatively safe from the organizational point of view but if the second of the options, in other words the BPR approach, is chosen the organization needs to be aware of the dangers involved in such radical approaches being employed without the framework or context of a whole organization development or improvement process.

DEFINING AND MANAGING PROCESSES

The second option for utilizing our knowledge of business processes is altogether more structured. First of all it involves defining the relevant business processes in a coherent and rigorous manner. This can be done in a variety of ways but the most successful method in our experience is called Process Quality Management (PQM). This technique is dealt with in detail in Chapter 6. We have used PQM hundreds of times in a wide variety of organizations. It is an extremely effective method when handled with knowledge and skill, but like so many things that sound simple, when it comes to using it successfully there is more to it than meets the eye.

We were once working with a multinational that had something of a fetish for doing work themselves, which in itself of course is no bad thing. On this occasion, however, we had run a two-day PQM workshop for the senior team and it had been very successful, so much so that they decided that they wanted to cascade the use of the technique down to the teams at the next level. The organization's improvement process co-ordinator had attended the programme we ran, had assisted us, and had now decided that he could run these follow-on sessions by himself. We advised him against it, saying that he should run at least a couple more with us before trying to do any on his own, but he would hear nothing of it. We received a rather mournful telephone call a couple of weeks later during which he explained, 'I started off really well, got them through the first two sessions no problem. I was just beginning to think that it was all a piece of cake when we got to the third session at about four o'clock and then the wheels fell off! ... Help!'

PQM involves the organization, a division or department defining its mission, or fundamental business purpose, and then the key success factors (KSF) that are individually necessary and collectively sufficient if the mission is to be achieved. There will be a maximum of eight KSFs. Having done this the next step is to define the business processes that currently exist and any new ones that will be needed for the attainment of the mission. Typically an organization will define between 20 and 30 separate processes. At this point the processes are rated in terms of importance and current effectiveness and an 'owner' is appointed for each of them. This decision is usually made on the basis of who has most to gain by the process performing well and most to lose if it doesn't. Those selected will almost always come from the group which defined the processes. At the organizational level, for example, this will be the directors and, possibly, senior managers.

The process owners are then responsible for working on improving the performance of the process. They must, of course, be given the appropriate authority and access to the necessary resources. The process owners must retain their existing executive roles and portfolios so there is no addition to the organization's head count.

This raises the question of how people can take on such significant additional responsibilities. People do sometimes argue that they have no time for extra work but the rationale here is that if the processes which drive the organization can be brought under control, unnecessary work will be eliminated and problems will be solved, time and other resources will then be freed up to do more effective work. In addition it is worth remembering that the process owner is not there to do all the improvement work but to be responsible for ensuring that it is done.

There are a number of ways that the process owner can approach the task, one of which is to use the Business Process Re-engineering methodology. Again it is important to note that not only will caution be needed but also co-ordination, if this is the chosen route, because an individual process owner who decides to use BPR without the understanding and support of the rest of the senior team will be in danger of causing havoc in the organization as a whole. Equally if all the process owners decided to use the approach simultaneously it would lead to the same result. Some of the techniques used in the improvement process are relatively safe, and even if for some reason they go wrong not too much damage will result, but techniques like BPR, because of their radical nature, need to be handled with much more caution.

PROCESS STRUCTURES

The third way of using our knowledge of business processes is in defining the organization structure and managing the organization itself. The way that organizations structure themselves has a key influence on their performance and, amazingly, most are structured in a way that actively hinders progress rather than helps it. This is because individual specialist departments so often operate almost entirely as 'functional drainpipes', seeming to think that they have a role, and a reason to exist, purely in their own right rather than realizing that their only value is as suppliers to their internal or external customers.

Structures based more on the business processes that exist can avoid this danger by creating work teams that contain all the relevant specialist skills and are responsible for the entirety of the process rather than just the part that is relevant to their technical speciality.

Organization structures should have a purpose, form should follow function, the structure should be designed to fit a particular set of objectives. Yet in the vast majority of cases it is simply treated as a matter of putting names into predetermined boxes on the organization chart, in other words as one insightful manager put it, 'form follows folk'!

Changing the organization structure to reflect the business processes can have far-reaching and dramatic results. An example of this comes from a medium-sized bottling company where functionalism was rife, production efficiencies were abysmal and everyone was far too busy to be interested in the customers who, as one director put it, 'have to fit in with the way we do things, after all it's for their own good'! The Managing Director realized that the way they were structured was one of the important impediments to their making progress with the existing improvement process and specifically his desire to use BPR, and so he asked us to help him reorganize which we did using the unique re-engineering methodology outlined below.

The task of re-engineering the organization structure starts from a blank sheet and involves a rigorous step-by-step process which commences with selecting the person or people to do the job. Structure is a clear responsibility of the top team, and ultimately the Chief Executive. One of the important tasks that they are paid for is to ensure that the structure in place is the one that best suits the organization's purpose and then to deploy people appropriately in the positions that need to be filled.

In our experience the Chief Executive must be involved in the process of making these decisions, with or without a small team of selected senior people which should number no more than four in all unless there are particularly pressing reasons for the whole of the senior team to be involved. The difficulty with this latter option is that if the full team is involved there is often an implied assumption that all of them have a legitimate role and this can prevent a full exploration of all of the possibilities since in certain circumstances some will 'see the writing on the wall' and may become negative and destructive.

Step two calls for a clarification of the ground rules that will apply during what is likely to be a series of three or four one-day meetings. The rules that need to be spelled out, understood and reinforced are first that form follows function as described above.

The second is that the work should be conducted with no preconceptions about the effectiveness, or lack of it, of the existing structure. The task is not to criticize or to support what is in place currently, but merely to ensure that the structure that is agreed is the best possible in terms of supporting and contributing to the achievement of the organization's mission.

Third it must be made absolutely clear that the exercise is concerned with the structure, not the names of the people who will occupy the positions within it. Once this is agreed the Chief Executive has the task of allocating people to jobs. One of the most limiting aspects of this kind of work are assumptions that are made about the levels of competence of existing incumbents.

The task at hand is to develop the most appropriate structure for the organization, not the 'least worst' one that is possible with the present situation and staff. The right structure may take a number of years, and more than one phase, to put in place fully but this is far better than implementing something that can only ever be sub-optimal, the structure is much too important and influential for this to be allowed to happen.

Fourth, the starting-point must be a blank sheet of paper. Most work on organization structure begins with a whole set of, usually conventional, assumptions about what can and should be, and involves a process of inserting names into pre-prepared boxes on an organization structure chart. This is a sure way of preventing an exploration of all of the possibilities any one of which might be precisely the correct one for the circumstances.

The final ground rule is that those involved should think creatively while engaged in the process as a way of ensuring that all the possibilities are explored.

The third step begins the work itself and involves asking the question, 'What do we want the structure to do for us?' We find that using the technique of brainstorming is the best way of eliciting the sort of comprehensive listing that is required at this stage. However, there is more to running such a meeting than simply saying, 'let's have a brainstorming session'. To get the most out of this important phase it is advisable to use a facilitator who has experience of the technique since most so-called brainstorming sessions are nothing of the sort.

Our experience of such meetings is that the list is likely to be quite lengthy, usually containing over 100 ideas and covering a wide range of issues. In accordance with the rules of brainstorming all of these ideas will have been recorded on flip charts and will have been posted round the room. What follows is a period of reflection and incubation so that the range and scale of the list can begin to be absorbed.

Step four involves discussing and agreeing the key characteristics that the structure is to be built round. In our experience there are likely to be between five and eight such characteristics which we call the fundamental design features. This discussion takes place with all the ideas in full view and needs to be rigorous since deciding on the key features is clearly a critical step. The debate at this stage is likely to be quite lengthy since a full consensus is required, and the number of times an issue has been raised is not necessarily any indication of its importance, so there is much more involved than counting up the number of mentions. Some people find this step quite difficult to conceptualize so alternative ways of describing it are either that these are the core building blocks on which the structure will be based, or that when the structure is agreed it will clearly reflect and have been based on these key features.

The fifth step involves evaluating the current structure in terms of these key characteristics, to list the different observations on flip charts and to post them round the room. The analysis should include areas both where the current structure meets the designated requirements and where it does not. The assessment needs to be done in a dispassionate way. It is quite normal to find that the present situation leaves a great deal to be desired when looked at in this way. Sometimes the current structure is seen to be doing nothing positive at all in meeting the requirements, but more commonly there will be a mixture of positive and negative points.

At this point the challenge is to look at the key characteristics and to think creatively about all the possible options that are available. Remember two things while engaged in this stage, first that the objective is to identify all of the possible options and second that names are not an issue. It is all too easy to discount possibilities on the basis of the current levels of ability of people within the organization and we should actively work to avoid being constrained in this way. Again, in our experience, a range of alternative possible structures emerge at this point, the minimum we have encountered is four and the maximum 23!

Step seven is the point at which the different options are evaluated rigorously, and in terms of the key characteristics. It is better to allow a period for incubation before this stage since the process of mulling over the possibilities is usually very productive. Again it is worth stressing that no names are involved at this stage since we are dealing only with the question of which structure best addresses the key characteristics that the organization wishes to build itself round. The reason for this is that there is a temptation to become distracted by worries about the organization's ability to handle one or another structure because it is different from what currently exists or because it appears that the skills do not currently exist to operate it successfully. Remember to resist the temptation to design sub-optimal structures because it may be difficult to manage the right one.

It is often at this stage that those involved are surprised as they come to realize that what they really want and need is a far cry from what they currently have. Step eight involves selecting the preferred option, not in the conventional sense of agreeing what 'boxes' will be needed under the Chief Executive's name but in the descriptive sense of the work that has been done so far. Much of the hard work has already been done, but considerable courage may be required still to put the new structure in place.

Step nine involves defining what the key issues are likely to be in managing the transition from where we are now to the new structure. In some cases this will present few difficulties while in others a plan will need to be devised which could take a considerable time to put in place. Organizations should not be put off by this. As has been said before, the way an organization is structured has a profound influence on the way that it operates, and is certainly far too important not to get right.

The result of using this process in the bottling company was the introduction of a structure that reflected the purpose of the organization, in other words its customers, and also the flow of work through the organization rather than functional specialisms. Customer Service directorates were established to replace the existing traditional ones of production, engineering, quality assurance and so on. These directors, who were the same people as before, were now responsible for the whole process of planning, production and delivery to their customer, as well as customer care.

At the start the idea of the new structure was not popular, to say the least. The Quality Assurance director, for example, complained that he had spent his business life developing his knowledge, a set of skills and credibility in his chosen field and now 'they' were taking it away from him. At the outset no one said a single word about the potential impact as far as the customer was concerned, the only comments were, either directly or implicitly, about the effect on 'my job' and 'my function' which was a comment on the depth of conditioning that we were dealing with.

Today, two years later, it is as if the new structure has always been in place. The customers, who have been surveyed, think that the whole idea is wonderful, the directors love the completeness of their role, and the employees, who are primarily concerned with different aspects of production, enjoy being part of customer teams. Productivity is now respectable and improving all the time, as are business results; last year was their best ever.

Developing the most appropriate way of structuring an organization should be seen as an important ingredient of any comprehensive Business Process Re-engineering project. Unless this is the case it is possible, even likely, that the new processes that are put in place will be undermined by the restrictions of the previous way of organizing, reporting relationships and so on. Business Process Management is an increasingly essential ingredient in the running of the modern organization. In our experience the task of helping people to redesign an organization's structure very often results in the recognition that a process-oriented way of organizing will best suit their needs, but this is not always the case. As with every aspect of re-engineering we should not make any prior assumptions.

NOTES

1. Taylor, F.W. (1911), *The Principles of Scientific Management*, New York: Harper & Row.

3 An Overview of Business Process Re-engineering

Here we deal with many of the initial questions that people want answers to before they commit themselves to the BPR approach. The format traces the typical sequence of questions and includes an outline of the main stages of a BPR project. Each stage is dealt with more completely in later chapters.

FINDING OUT ABOUT BPR

One of the early questions that people ask is how can they obtain an objective view of what BPR is. They may well have read a few articles on the subject which have whetted their appetite, but have found that since most of the articles revolve around case histories it can be difficult to relate the practice of the technique to their own organization. They say that it looks exciting and sounds like a good idea, certainly if the reported results are real, but they want to know how they can learn about it properly and assess whether it is appropriate for their particular circumstances.

If it is an individual who is doing some preliminary investigation of the subject there are three main avenues. A number of books have been written on the subject of BPR, and these of course can provide information, though this is the first 'practical guide' to the subject as far as we are aware; some relevant texts are listed and described in the 'Further Reading' section on pages 155–56. A second option is to contact organizations who have experience of having re-engineered some of their processes. Such organizations are usually very willing to display their successes but can sometimes overstate them and omit to mention the things that they did not do so well. The best single option, however, is to attend a training workshop on the subject.

If the senior management team wishes to explore the possibilities, there is little doubt that an in-house executive briefing is by far the best approach since it can be designed specifically for the organization in question, and with the purpose of developing a consensus among the senior team as to the most appropriate way ahead. There are many situations in which using BPR would be inappropriate, so such events must not simply put pressure on people to agree to the approach, they must be designed as a genuine exploration of the technique and its applicability in the organization in question. Typically the agenda of such a session, which would last for a day would include the following topics:

- The challenges currently facing organizations and the consequent need for change and the tools and techniques to help us manage change successfully.
- The limitations of traditional functional approaches to management and the potential of new concepts of process management. The practicalities of managing in this way.
- A clarification of BPR and discussion of how this tool differs from other approaches notably philosophies of continuous improvement such as Total Quality.
- A description and discussion about the key enablers of BPR; in other words the important levers that can allow truly radical ideas to work.
- An explanation of how BPR should be seen as part of a bigger whole which should be the all-encompassing process that frames and defines everything the organization is and does.
- A presentation of the correct way to approach BPR including each of the necessary steps and examples from organizations that have succeeded and others that have fallen into the many traps that await the unwary.
- The likely benefits that can be expected in different environments and a frank and realistic assessment of the potential barriers that will need to be overcome if they are to be achieved.
- The key roles that are needed to support a BPR project together with a description of the different personal characteristics that are helpful in the different tasks.
- The need for the senior team of the organization to form a steering group and a discussion of the important roles that this group needs to understand and be responsible for.
- An explanation and discussion of a template project plan for the introduction of BPR into the organization.
- Presentation and discussion on some of the key organizational issues that will need to be addressed such as how to deal with the possibility of staff reductions, how to communicate the scale of the likely changes, how much access to information to allow to staff especially during the re-engineering process.

- How to manage the changes that will be required when implementing the new process, including the need to identify and manage the many possible 'knock-on' effects.

DO WE REALLY NEED BPR?

Many organizations are interested in the potential gains that can be forthcoming as a result of BPR projects but express concern and anxiety about the potential disruption that might be caused. Typically organizations that respond in this way will be, or will perceive themselves to be, performing at least adequately at the moment. They will not see their viability being under serious threat for reasons of either internal effectiveness or competitive position.

This stance may or may not reflect an accurate interpretation of the situation in which they find themselves, but such organizations will often say things like: 'We are performing satisfactorily at the moment. Of course we could do better and we are interested in the potential that BPR seems to offer, but would it really be sensible of us to rock the boat at this stage? After all BPR is not about a pleasant gentle rocking, it's about hitting ourselves with a tidal wave! It could cause us to capsize.'

There is, in our experience, no single and universally correct answer to this often asked question, but there are a few relevant points that should be made and that might be of use to people who are thinking this way. The first concerns the accuracy of the assessment of current performance and future threats, or the lack of them. Of course there are organizations that are performing extremely well and whose position in or dominance of the market-place, for whatever reason, seems secure, even inviolable, but their numbers are declining very quickly. There are many more organizations that think they are in this situation but are not, and who do not have the ability or in some cases the willingness to see it.

Any organization that finds itself thinking this way should institute an even more rigorous assessment of its current and potential future situation preferably using an orderly methodology such as a SWOT (strengths, weaknesses, opportunities and threats) analysis. If this process leads to the same conclusion then some form of external assessment should be sought. This may seem to be excessive but, in our experience, there is far more chance of an organization deluding itself in this regard than there is that of it really being safe and secure.

Continuing with the sailing metaphor, an organization that is to succeed with BPR requires a firm, courageous and steady hand on the tiller so those organizations that are concerned about whether or not they should 'rock the boat' need to ask themselves whether they are likely to have the necessary resolve to see the project through to the end. It is better not to start than to begin and then falter.

CAN BPR BE USED BY 'CARING' ORGANIZATIONS?

BPR is generally and justifiably perceived as a 'hard-nosed' technique and it is difficult to see how it could be otherwise bearing in mind what it is trying to achieve. Its reputation in this regard is often misunderstood, but equally can cause concern.

Some organizations can accurately be called 'caring', others think of themselves in this way but are not. Both of these categories, however, are quite likely to ask about the compatibility or otherwise of the approach on the one hand and their organizational philosophy and values on the other.

To answer this question it is necessary first to establish that being a caring organization should not imply any sense of weakness or sentimentality. True caring organizations recognize that their most precious asset is their employees; therefore they will be wise to, look after this resource skilfully and sensitively, if they want it to work well for them and to play its part in optimizing business performance. Such organizations do not, however, avoid potentially difficult 'people' issues, they confront them; they do not carry excess in any of the different types of resource that they employ, including the human one. They recognize that to carry unnecessary resources for anything but well-considered strategic reasons amounts to dereliction of duty, and if the resources concerned happen to be human, an insult to those involved in performing what have been recognized as unnecessary tasks. Caring organizations go to great lengths to ensure that they meet these challenges in an appropriately sensitive and generous manner and recognize that the need for change is rarely the fault of the resources that are affected.

In the light of the above it is clear that there is no fundamental incompatibility that should prevent caring organizations from using BPR and achieving the gains that are possible. In fact, because such organizations do care for their people they are more likely to consider the potential consequences and to plan carefully for them and by so doing they give themselves a better chance of success through using the technique.

HOW DO YOU HANDLE THE 'PEOPLE' ISSUES?

It is almost inevitable that a BPR project will raise issues concerning the staff who are involved in the process at the start. The questions are usually concerning what to do with the people whose jobs are no longer required with the new process. Understandably it is this issue that causes the most soul searching among senior people before and also during the BPR project and it is certainly a very commonly asked question. Of course there is no one universally appropriate response but again there are a number of guidelines which can help.

The first and probably the most important piece of advice for the senior team is that they should take particular care in considering the potential issues and, broadly speaking, the stance they intend to take before commencing the project. Far too many organizations fail to do this and then find themselves trapped by the situation as it develops; staff begin to ask searching questions about the possible consequences of BPR for them and their jobs and why they should become involved in something that could be instrumental in losing them their livelihood.

The last thing that any senior management wants is to be trying to answer such emotionally laden questions 'off the cuff', and it is almost as bad to plead for time to think. If the issues have not been thought through rigorously and a clear, explicable and defensible position developed the temptation is to 'massage' the truth which of course is only ever a short-term palliative and always leads to trouble in the end. As always it is better to plan for this occurrence before the event and thereby prevent many of the problems that will inevitably arise otherwise.

There are always a range of options when it comes to dealing with the matter of jobs that are made redundant by the improvement process and it is far better to have developed a clear approach ahead of time. Some organizations choose to guarantee that there will be no loss of jobs but state that everyone must be prepared to be redeployed. The argument here is generally that the process of re-engineering should make the organization more competitive and so enable it to improve its market share and that the spare staff can be utilized to help this happen. Alternatively such companies choose to reduce their numbers by the normal process of attrition, that is, retirements and turnover, and are prepared for the fact that such an approach will mean that the gains made will take a lot longer to be realized.

Other organizations accept that there will be redundancies but agree that they will be handled on a voluntary basis. This approach has the advantage of reducing the amount of fear and apprehension that so often surrounds any process of change, and certainly one as radical as BPR. The disadvantage, however, is that the organization has no control over who takes up the offer, and it is often the most talented and self-assured staff who have the confidence to take the risk, and the less marketable people are the ones that stay.

The third option is to accept that redundancies are likely and that they should be confronted directly. Many organizations that take this approach will make sure that the redundancy packages offered are generous enough to avoid at least some of the negative associations of this approach.

At least part of the gains to be made by BPR are likely to be in the form of savings in people costs so the organization should have its position worked out ahead of time. In one organization we worked with, the senior team, despite the pressure we put on them, were not prepared to do this. They made all sorts of excuses one of which was that they saw little purpose in working out what they would do in theory, they were practical people and preferred to deal with real situations. We were tempted to quote the old adage, 'show me a "practical" person and I'll show you an amateur' but we desisted!

They were very anxious to get on with some real re-engineering. This part of the project actually went well and the newly designed process which was presented was clearly better in terms of customer satisfaction as well as cost-effectiveness. The difficulties began when they realized first that for them to reap the benefit involved losing 30 of the 45 jobs it currently took to perform the process, and second that they were not prepared to 'bite this bullet'. Again there were all sorts of excuses, from 'it's not our culture' to 'we'll redeploy productively elsewhere (but we don't know where)'.

An interesting additional outcome was that the company concerned began to attract criticism from its parent for spending so much time, effort and money on a project which seemed to have achieved so little. This took more time and effort to deal with as it meandered into an argument about whether BPR worked or not. It was an unfortunate example of the common syndrome that in such situations it is always the wrong subject that gets the blame, in this case BPR rather than poor management!

WHAT CAN GO WRONG?

Quite understandably and rightly many organizations want to know what can go wrong before they start with such a radical approach. The honest answer to the question is that everything can go wrong and that equally nothing needs to. It comes back to the basic premiss of this book, which based on our extensive experience, and that of others, is that if such projects are well planned and handled with skill and care nothing need go wrong. Enough is now known about the potential hazards to be able to avoid them if this experience is used wisely.

SUCCESS RATES WITH BPR

Another question that is commonly asked at the outset concerns the success and failure rates of organizations that attempt BPR projects. There is nothing different in BPR as far as this is concerned. It is no more a 'magic wand' than anything else. The answer to the question is that organizations that do it properly by using a robust methodology, appropriately knowledgeable and skilled resources and by managing the change process with care, courage and commitment always succeed with the technique. On the other hand those organizations that treat it as the latest flavour of the month, that think it is easy and can be done without skilled resources and that treat it as a peripheral issue always fail – and, incidentally, always blame the technique.

The literature on the subject is beginning to indicate that there are more organizations in the latter than the former category, but this is not surprising since it has been the case with every significant managerial and organizational innovation, certainly in the past 30 years, and probably well before that. Organizations should not be dissuaded because of this, simply warned that BPR is serious work which requires serious and intelligent thought, commitment, resourcing and effort.

BPR PROJECT STAGES

WHEN SHOULD WE START?

In a world of change something is always happening that makes it the 'wrong' time to start any initiative, let alone one as radical in its implications as BPR. We have lost count of the number and range of reasons that have been put forward to us for delaying the start of a whole range of initiatives, not just BPR. For the most part, these arguments are raised for genuine reasons and out of real concern. It is relatively rare that the reasoning put forward is an obvious excuse and an avoidance tactic, though it does happen from time to time.

The issue then is whether even well-meaning reasons for delay are valid, and the answer, basically, is that they are not. As is the case with all such statements, there will clearly be exceptions to the rule, but as generalizations go it is a good one. As mentioned above in the world as it is today there is no such thing as the 'right time', there will always be a hundred and one reasons for delay, so if there is no 'right time' why not start now; remember as Edward Young said some 250 years ago, 'procrastination is the thief of time'.

HOW DO YOU START?

Having explored the subject and decided to proceed, the next question concerns how to start. The first step involves defining the processes that are used in the organization. This is done by the full senior team in a Process Quality Management (PQM) workshop which is fully described in Chapter 6. BPR can be used at a number of levels, for example the entire organization, a business unit, a division, or even a main function, and a clear decision on the relevant level needs to be made at the outset. The full senior team of the organization, or the part chosen, must take part in the PQM event, and it should not be run until this is possible. One of the outputs of the workshop is a list of the business processes used in the organization, prioritized in terms of their importance and current effectiveness.

HOW DO YOU SELECT A PROCESS FOR RE-ENGINEERING?

The next step is to decide which process to work on and this decision should be made on the basis of the impact that substantial improvement would have on the external customer, the strategic relevance of the process especially in terms of current competitor performance, the impact that massively changing the process would have on other processes in the organization and the present performance of the process. These questions need to be debated rigorously and appropriate decisions made since it is very unwise to attempt too much too soon. In large organizations a few BPR projects, say three or four, can be worked on simultaneously, but normally one or two projects would be the maximum to be involved with at any one time.

WHAT RESOURCES ARE NEEDED TO SUPPORT A BPR PROJECT?

The resourcing of BPR projects is the next question that needs to be answered since a number of decisions have to be made at this point. First a re-engineering team that consists of appropriate balance of seniority needs to be appointed. If the team is too junior it may lack vision and credibility whereas if it is too senior it may lack the necessary detailed knowledge of the process in question. The team should normally comprise between five and seven members. Within the team it is always best to have one or two who are not directly involved in the process, maybe IT or human resource (HR) professionals, external consultants, or simply individuals who have a high level of imagination and creativity.

Whether or not to employ consultants to assist is also an issue that needs to be addressed at this stage. There is little doubt that knowledgeable and skilful external support can be of great use in conducting BPR projects. However, those consultants chosen should be able to demonstrate a track record in this kind of work, and their philosophy should be one of developing internal resources to the point where the knowledge and skills exist in-house. There are already far too many examples of large consultancies selling huge assignments for themselves to do the re-engineering rather than to assist internal resources to do it. Such consultancies are cynical in the extreme, and one has to say that organizations that agree to such assignments are either very gullible, very naive about organizational dynamics, or just plain stupid with more money than sense!

The key roles that are needed to support a BPR project include a steering group, which should be the senior management team, a co-ordinator who pulls together the administrative requirements, a process owner selected by the top team, a facilitator who understands the methodology as well as possessing facilitative skills, a team leader and, as is mentioned above, the re-engineering team itself.

An important part of the resourcing requirement is that the senior team give active support to the process and are prepared to give the required amount of time to the team right from the start of the project.

The final part of the resourcing requirement is the training needed in the different skills, tools and techniques that will be used in the process of re-engineering. These must not be underestimated and include problem-solving and facilitative skills, as well as training in the concepts, principles and practices of BPR. For the most part such training is best conducted in 'real time' as people need to use a particular technique to get to the next stage of the process.

HOW LONG DOES A BPR PROJECT TAKE?

The next question refers to the length of time it takes to re-engineer a process. This will obviously depend on a number of things such as the intensity with which the team works, whether they will be working on a full- or a part-time basis on the project, as well as the underlying complexity of the process itself. As a guideline if the process is of moderate size and complexity and the team meets once every two weeks for half a day and does any necessary follow-up work and data collection in the interim, six months to completion of the project is usual, excluding any time that might be needed for things like specially designed software if this is necessary.

Once the conceptual side of the re-engineering has been completed and a new process has been designed and agreed the challenge becomes one of managing the change and this can often be the most complicated and difficult part of the whole exercise. Issues such as whether to prototype the new process or not, whether to run it in parallel for a while are relatively easy decisions to make compared to those concerning the people such as managers, employees, suppliers and customers both internal and external, who will be affected in one way or another.

There are many issues to think about when considering a BPR project, and there are certainly many traps awaiting the unwary and the unprepared. However, the gains resulting from BPR are enormous and well worth the care, attention, commitment and investment that is needed to make the venture a real success.

4 Requirements for Success

In this chapter we will deal with the foundations that are necessary for success with BPR, including setting the behavioural framework. These are often the less tangible but none the less important factors that will inevitably damage the programme if they are not handled well. Because these issues are so important it is rather surprising that they seem largely to have been omitted from other texts on this subject.

THE ROLE OF SENIOR MANAGEMENT

The first issue concerns the role of senior management. The word commitment, and specifically the phrase 'top management commitment' is so overworked, so misunderstood and often so poorly practised that it has precious little meaning any more, let alone credibility. Its claimed existence is used as an excuse by many senior people to ignore what happens thereafter; while its absence is blamed by everyone else to explain why it is not worth starting or why things are not going well. Because of this it will be much more useful to examine the role of top management without using either the word or the phrase.

It is the job of senior management to set clearly the direction of an organization and to communicate this to employees. It is also their role to develop strategies that will help the organization on its journey. Top managers, whether they like it or not, have a large influence on the behavioural standards and norms that prevail at all levels of their particular company. Any significant shifts in direction, strategy or policy will need to be explained to people in the organization if they are to be able to understand and then play their part.

Of course different issues will have different levels of significance and importance attached to them, and members of staff who are constantly trying to interpret clues as to the really important issues will make their own judgements. The relative importance of the issue will be judged by employees, not on the length of the memo that explains it, not on the impassioned language, not even on the protestations of undying '--------------------'! People are too smart for that, they have a much more accurate gauge, they watch what the senior people actually do rather than what they talk about; simple, and highly effective.

The members of the re-engineering team will also need visible support and guidance. BPR is about radical change of the kind which will never have been experienced in the organization before. Because of this the team will need regular reassurance that senior management recognize not only the extent of the likely changes but also their implications, and that they are prepared to go through with and support the project to the full. Some teams also need regular encouragement from the top, especially in the early stages, to think creatively and not limit themselves in any way.

Generally speaking senior management will not be members of the re-engineering team and so they should arrange regular review meetings to enable them to show visible support. It is also very effective if they make it their business to 'bump into' team members occasionally and to use this opportunity to reinforce their encouragement and support. Such behaviours have infinitely more effect than memos or second-hand messages.

A further role of the top team, which is obvious but needs stating, is that they must make it their business to develop a thorough understanding of what BPR is about and the likely consequences of choosing to use this tool. Already there are far too many examples of senior managers starting BPR projects in their organizations without any real understanding because it has become 'the thing to do', only to find that they are unprepared to handle the complexities of radical change either organizationally or in terms of human resources.

Since the scale of the changes can be massive the senior team must be prepared for them and, wherever possible, manage them throughout the course of the project. Changes of the kind which are sometimes possible with BPR can be quite a shock to senior managers, let alone others, and it is a responsibility of the members of the senior team to decide what they want the organization to get out of BPR, and what sort of an organization it will be after the BPR projects have been completed. They will need to keep this picture clearly in mind and they should share this vision with others in the organization who are involved, affected or simply interested.

UNDERSTANDING BPR IN RELATION TO OTHER INITIATIVES

A part of understanding what BPR is concerns its relationship with other initiatives. A common area of misunderstanding is BPR and process improvement; they are not the same. Process improvement is working on improvement continuously and achieving gains on a regular basis, albeit usually gains of a relatively small nature, whereas BPR is achieving massive gains in one fell swoop. Because of the scale of benefits that BPR can generate and because it is a new technique, some people have hailed it as a replacement for existing initiatives which, of course, it is not. BPR is a tool within the whole improvement process which in its turn should, ideally, be based on the application of the tools and techniques of Total Quality.

Organizations need to be crystal clear about this if they are not to find themselves at best confused and at worst in serious difficulties. The evidence suggests that, though widely used, 'Total Quality' is probably not a very good term to use in describing the whole process since it often leads to misunderstandings. Nowadays we usually advise our clients to avoid the term while still using the principles and practices that underpin it. None the less it is the commonly used title of a process that is designed to be a complete and coherent way of running an organization and so, for the purpose of the discussion here, we will use it.

Total Quality, as a way of running all aspects of an organization recognizes that organizations need to have a sound set of foundations first consisting of a set of shared behaviours, or a philosophy of working, and second a clearly enunciated mission or fundamental business purpose. It also emphasizes the need to ensure that the organizational infrastructure is healthy enough to support the process of change that is involved. Second, Total Quality involves using the principles and practices that underpin it in doing every piece of work in the organization. Total Quality based on a set of concepts that are undeniable and, importantly, it provides the necessary tools and techniques for people in organizations to turn the theory into practice.

By no stretch of the imagination can BPR be seen in this light. It is not designed to be an integrated way of running an organization and it cannot fulfil this function. What it can and does provide is an immensely effective tool to be used within a comprehensive, conceptual, organization development framework.

BPR projects must dovetail with other activities and techniques that are used within the whole process and this should be understood in the organization. This has often been neglected by organizations, to the detriment of the process and also the understanding of the employees who can easily become confused about where BPR fits, because it is so radical, and because it is different in kind from most of the other tools that are likely to be in use.

BPR should not be used indiscriminately, but in selected areas where it is clear either that there is very significant room for improvement, where competitors are 'stealing a march', or where real competitive advantage can be gained by the sort of quantum leap that BPR can offer. Because BPR needs to be used strategically and in a targeted fashion there should always be a rigorous discussion about which of the many tools available will be the most appropriate to exploit any area of potential improvement. BPR will not be used in every eventuality, and equally it will be used in some.

After a BPR project has been completed the process of continuous improvement should take over, with those who work with the process being responsible, both individually and collectively, for ensuring that it is kept up to date, that improvement opportunities are identified and worked on and that any legitimate changes in the requirements of the customers of the process are accommodated and built in.

BPR does not stand alone. Rather it links with the many tools of continuous improvement such as Statistical Process Control, the In-Department Evaluation of Activity (IDEA) and Quality Circles.

COMMUNICATING TO STAFF

To embark on BPR is a significant strategic decision and so it needs explaining to people in the organization not least because they are likely to be fearful of the implications anyway and will be more so in the absence of any explanation. This requirement presents significant difficulties in the minds of many senior people at the outset. BPR is about trying to create change and improvement on a scale probably not seen in the organization before, and a clear implication of this is the possibility, even likelihood, of loss of jobs.

Understandably many senior managers are reluctant to make public announcements that are likely to have a detrimental effect on the motivation and morale of their employees and so the question debated by many is how open to be in briefing the people in the organization. This often becomes a long, circular and ultimately unsatisfactory discussion because the right questions have not been discussed and appropriate policies agreed beforehand.

DEVELOPING A POLICY FOR JOB LOSSES

A successfully re-engineered process will either achieve the same or more output with significantly less resource or will achieve significantly more output with the same resource. Of the two the first is much more likely. Management then must face the fact that fewer people are going to be needed to support the organization's present level of business. This and the consequent improvement in results is why a BPR approach was selected in the first place. Management know that the issue exists before they start and so equally they should discuss and agree their approach to it before they start.

There are three main options that need to be discussed, discounting a fourth, which is to lie. Many organizations actually choose this option either wittingly or unwittingly, but it never works because in an organizational context too many people have good individual and collective memories for the lie to be carried off successfully. Lying is not worth the effort and difficulties involved in trying to rectify matters once the lie has been discovered.

Assuming that the organization is going to communicate honestly, the first possibility is to guarantee that there will be no redundancies as a result of the re-engineering projects. This is obviously the best option as far as the ease of managing the situation is concerned since it takes what is probably the main, though not the only, fear out of the equation. Such a guarantee will only be possible if the organization is in a position of significant growth or potential growth, or if people can be redeployed either within the organization or another part of the group.

This option will invariably require a comprehensive programme of reinduction, retraining and possibly relocation so it is not without its costs and its difficulties, but it remains the least controversial possibility as far as dealing with staff is concerned. However, the organization needs to be very confident of its ability to deploy the spare resources productively before taking this option.

A few years ago IBM with its famous 'no layoffs' policy realized that owing to a range of improvements that had been made in its manufacturing process it was substantially overmanned in this area. They redeployed thousands of people into sales, marketing and software design and spent millions training them. In the end, however, they simply had to change the policy, which was one of the most cherished parts of the IBM tradition. They would not have survived otherwise.

A significant part of the financial gain that is possible through using BPR is likely to emanate from reductions in head count, so organizations have to be honest with themselves if they take this option. It will be no good complaining that BPR did not produce the results if this option is chosen and the other parts of the equation do not work out. It is our practice therefore to press for a rigorous 'accounting' system when this option is selected so that no one is in any doubt as to the real results of the BPR project itself as opposed to the effects of management decisions about how to handle the potential benefits.

The second possibility is for management to decide that if there are to be job losses they will be dealt with by a combination of voluntary redundancy, early retirement and redeployment rather than recruitment; in other words no compulsory redundancy. This way of dealing with the situation has a considerable appeal but it also has one or two disadvantages.

On the plus side there is no doubt that this option removes much of the fear that always accompanies change which involves the spectre of redundancy. Somewhat surprisingly in view of the general reduction in the number of available jobs nowadays, offers of voluntary redundancy are usually well-subscribed. Easier to understand are the applications for early retirement, especially if the terms are reasonably generous which they often are, but this is a very expensive option from the organization's point of view.

The first negative implication of this approach is that it is often the most confident and able employees who choose to leave, and there is precious little that the organization can do to prevent this if such people apply and are determined. Second there is always the possibility that not enough volunteers will be forthcoming, in which case the organization either has to increase the terms of the offer, accept that the benefits will take longer to be realized or to renege on its commitment, none of which are particularly attractive. Third, whether voluntary or not, the word redundancy always seems to evoke considerable passion among employees and needs to be managed positively if the organization is not to be damaged by it.

The third possible approach is for the organization to develop a programme of compulsory redundancy. From the organization's point of view, in the long term this is likely to be the most beneficial option since, if managed successfully, it ensures that the benefits are gained sooner rather than later and that the most valuable people are retained.

The more difficult aspects of this option are largely obvious but need to be spelt out for the sake of completeness. First, the spectre of compulsory redundancy has always been frightening to most people even in times of full employment. In today's world it is even more so with jobs being much harder to find and there being no realistic possibility of a return to the full employment years of only two decades ago. Fear affects people profoundly and whereas some will argue that it concentrates the mind and spurs people on, for others it can be and often is very debilitating.

Second, the organization invariably is blamed, and often vilified for adopting such a course of action, however generous it is in its settlement terms, and the bad feeling can seriously affect performance for a period of time. It is remarkable how often people who have been recognized as poor performers by their colleagues, who have been the subject of discontent and covert criticism and who have been the butt of often cruel private jokes suddenly become 'hard done by triers' who deserved much better than to be made redundant and 'thrown out on the street' by this unfeeling organization.

Third, unless the organization adopts the unwise course of having outside consultants undertake the whole of the re-engineering process for them, rather than use them to provide a structure, the tools, techniques and facilitation, it can be problematic getting people to play their full part in the process and to think imaginatively and radically. Certainly in these circumstances skilled management and charismatic leadership is required, the first to keep the process on track and the second to provide the necessary sense of vision and purpose.

Finally, compulsory redundancy usually affects those that stay just as much as those that go, and in some cases more so. This fact is one that all too often escapes the attention of organizations who spend much time and effort developing sound and generous redundancy packages but fail to address the issue of the needs of those that remain nearly as systematically and carefully. It seems as if the assumption is that these people will be so grateful to remain employed that no particular effort is required. This is a huge error of judgement when it happens and is such a significant issue that it is specifically dealt with in Chapter 11 since special knowledge and skills are needed to handle such occurrences successfully.

Our purpose here is not to state definitively the correct approach but to emphasize first that it is a clear and inescapable responsibility of the senior team to develop a policy concerning possible job losses as a result of using a BPR approach, and that not to do so at the outset will almost invariably lead to difficulties, embarrassments and losses of credibility. Second, we emphasize that there are a number of different routes that are possible, any one of which could be correct for a particular organization at a particular time.

THE ONGOING NEED TO MANAGE CHANGE

Another issue that is better debated and communicated at the outset concerns the organization's views about change. Although we all live in a world of change it presents different challenges in different time-scales to organizations. For some it is an immediate imperative for survival whereas in others there is more time to think and consider different approaches. Many, if not most, people are discomfited by the need for change and so a senior team is wise to diagnose the situation in their particular field, to explain it carefully to staff and to outline their response to this assessment at least in general terms.

Ambrose Bierce once defined the word 'peace' as 'a state that exists between two periods of war'! In rather the same vein, for all the talk about us living in a world where change is the only constant, most people seem to treat it as something distinct and finite that happens between two periods of *status quo*. Such treatment inevitably leads to a situation where many people go through the anxieties associated with organizational changes programmes or processes each and every time these changes happen. Anxiety resulting from impending change, as we know, is difficult to handle and often has a negative effect on performance at least in the short term.

BPR is unashamedly about change, even to the point of adopting a philosophy of 'if it isn't broken, break it' rather than the traditional conventional wisdom that tells us to leave well alone. A good opportunity exists at the start to begin a process of re-education that is designed to do two things. The first is to get people to understand that the management of change is a constant requirement rather than something that happens periodically.

Second, it will be well worth while building at the start a process designed to get people to look forward to it and to enjoy it. One of the constant difficulties encountered by anyone who is in the business of managing change for improvement is that whereas everyone can see in fine detail both why others should change and what it is that they should be changing to, when the question is turned on to them, all of a sudden it becomes a criticism, a threat and even an insult; after all, as people say, 'we are all doing our best are we not, and no one can do more than that!'

This attitude is very common and entirely inappropriate. We need to be training, developing and encouraging our people to be active in the search for personal improvement on a continuous basis. Working smarter, not harder, is the challenge that faces every one of us. As a part of this organizations need to change their approach to recognition to one which gives full and public recognition to individuals and teams that have improved, from however low a base, and away from only recognizing high performers.

Any organization that wishes to survive and succeed in today's environment needs to be working on improvement constantly, and to be doing so in an orderly way using an appropriate mixture of the many tools and techniques that have been developed to assist the process. As we now know BPR is one of the available tools but it needs to be positioned correctly and supported appropriately if it is to yield the full potential of the benefits that it can generate.

5 Roles and Resources

A number of different roles are needed to support a BPR project, also a range of resources that will typically be required and these issues are discussed in detail in this chapter. The six key roles that need to be understood are those of the process owner, the team leader, facilitator, team member, external consultant and coordinator.

PROCESS OWNER

The idea of someone being designated to 'own' a business process is relatively new and for many people it takes some getting used to. The process owner has responsibility for the performance of the process in question and since processes flow through the organization this implies a cross-functional responsibility which is indeed the case.

Owning a process is very different to managing a department or function. A manager ultimately is responsible for the efficiency and effectiveness of the day-to-day activities that make up the work of the individual department. He or she should develop a deep and accurate understanding of the requirements of the customers of the section or department to ensure that the right work is being done and then manage the people who are doing the work in a way that makes sure it is carried out efficiently. Unfortunately it is often only the second element that receives any attention, which leads to so many departments doing the wrong work but doing it very well. The line manager is concerned with a part of the whole process and is looking at day-to-day performance.

On the other hand the process owner is concerned with measuring and improving the effectiveness of the entire process. The process owner's role, therefore, does not involve managing the day-to-day routine of each, or any, of the parts of the process, it involves doing whatever is necessary to be able to guarantee that the whole process and each of its constituent parts are effective, efficient and adaptable.

Effectiveness at the macro-level involves being clear about the requirements of the end customer and the legitimacy of these requirements, including whether or not they could be delivered in a different way or by different people and processes. At the micro-level effectiveness concerns all of the internal customer interfaces, ensuring that requirements are discussed rigorously and that the possibilities of delivering these requirements in different and better ways are fully considered. In this way the process owner is making sure that the purpose of the process is valid and that those engaged in its delivery are doing the right work.

Efficiency, in other words doing things right, is primarily the responsibility of the department manager, but the process owner has an obvious interest in it and has the responsibility for ensuring efficient working at the boundaries between departments which is where so many problems seem to occur. The process owner will be particularly concerned to ensure that appropriate measures of performance are in place at different stages of the process in question, whether these be within the departments involved or at the interfaces between them.

Adaptability is the third essential. Efficiency and effectiveness have long been recognized as key words but recognizing the importance of adaptability is much more recent. Many processes in organizations were debated thoroughly when they were introduced, and indeed were both effective and efficient, yet today they deliver outputs that still may be efficient, but certainly are not effective. The problem was that they were introduced at a time when change was not happening at such a rate as it is today. In the past little thought was given to the need for adaptability. It was assumed either openly or tacitly that once the system had been designed and implemented all that was needed was for managers to keep it running smoothly.

Today processes, if they are to serve their purpose well, cannot be 'bedded in concrete' as was the case in the past. It is both disruptive and costly to constantly have to 'dig up' processes and build them differently. In the modern business world recognizing that change will happen and that it can and should be accommodated is a key element in the design of robust business processes.

The owner is responsible for improving the performance of the whole process, and when it comes to the practicalities of working on improvement there is usually a good case for breaking down large processes into more easily handled sub-processes and for making selected people responsible for them under the leadership of the process owner. We should be quite clear that the idea of process ownership does not replace the existing organization structure, rather it operates like a matrix. The sub-processes will not necessarily follow and equate to departmental responsibilities, it is most likely that they too will be of a cross-functional nature.

With any such arrangement great care is needed to avoid unproductive conflict; since managers will be made accountable to other managers not in their function, at least for the effectiveness and ongoing improvement of their part of the process. The organization needs to be both clear and explicit in its definition of the responsibilities and authorities involved, and it is also useful to have a clear 'appeals procedure' for use in the event of intractable differences of opinion.

The role of the process owner needs to be both clarified and legitimized in most circumstances. Unless this is done the power of the functional hierarchy is likely to prevail, and in many organizations this frequently means a too rigid adherence to the *status quo*. All too often attempts to introduce process improvement have failed or barely got off the ground because the organization has failed to define the responsibilities and authorities clearly enough, and has not supported the process owners in their work, especially in the early stages.

SELECTING A PROCESS OWNER

At first glance it appears almost inevitable that more people would be required to fill these roles but in fact this is not the case since process ownership is an additional responsibility which is given to those selected. There are a number of important guidelines for the selection process, the first of which concerns process knowledge. The owner of a process obviously needs to develop a deep understanding of it. Because of this need it is likely that the person designated as owner will currently be managing one of the elements within the process, and it is by no means a bad starting-point to ask the question, who has most to gain by the process working well and most to lose if it is ineffective? This could be the person who manages the work that makes up most of the process, or it could be the person who manages the final delivery to the primary customer.

A second selection guideline concerns the power to influence and change. The process owner must be someone who commands the respect of those who are managing the different parts and someone who has the authority to make changes. This authority will be partly that vested in the person by the organization but, probably more importantly, it will be personal. This is necessary for a range of reasons but particularly because any changes will be introduced from outside the 'normal' executive line structure, and a greater danger exists of interfunctional squabbles breaking out unless the owner has credibility in both the professional and personal senses.

The third criterion that should be taken into account in selecting process owners is their ability as facilitators. Facilitators are agents of change, they work with individuals and groups on many different aspects of improvement. They normally have no direct line reporting relationship with those they are assisting, so they need a range of skills that do not rely purely on position or power in order to achieve their goals; in other words the ability to say 'do it because I say so!'

Skilful process owners recognize the importance of ownership, not for themselves but among those that work with the process day in, day out. Because of this facilitative skills are required that develop a willingness, and indeed a hunger, for working on process improvement in whatever way among those who are involved. The owner rarely will have either the time or the detailed knowledge of the process to do the work alone and it is therefore invaluable if process owners are trained in facilitation, and they put the skills to good use.

Fourth, the people chosen need to be enthusiastic about this additional responsibility. Little will be gained if the person chosen is not prepared to spend time and effort on understanding the process and then galvanizing people to work on improving it. Enthusiasm, as we all know, is infectious and can be invaluable in overcoming many of the initial fears that people have when working on change, especially change as radical as is the case with re-engineering.

The ownership of high-level, organization-wide processes will almost always be given to directors who, because of their position, should be able to take a 'helicopter' view, but the other criteria outlined here are essential if the job is to be performed successfully.

The responsibility for process ownership should always be made part of the job descriptions of those involved and the subject should be reviewed and discussed as a part of the performance appraisal system. This is more than a trivial administrative point since experience shows that there is far more chance of the matter receiving its due measure of importance if it is dealt with in this way. If it is not there is a danger that it is treated as an afterthought to be fitted in when there is time, which as we all know is never.

TEAM LEADER

The second role that we need to understand is that of the team leader for a BPR project. There is no doubt that the re-engineering process is a task best handled by a carefully selected group and that the designated leader is in a particularly influential position. There is some debate about whether a BPR project should be handled on a full- or part-time basis and this has a bearing on the team leader role. In our experience organizing the activity on a part-time basis is more successful. We find that this increases the level of creativity of the group and also ensures that those involved do not either physically or emotionally separate themselves from the rest of the organization and thereby cause fear and alienation among the other employees.

As far as the team leader is concerned the project being a part-time responsibility means that the best potential candidates can be selected without running the risk of prejudicing the day-to-day management of the operation. With full-time projects this issue is always significant and often results in the 'B' team being selected with obvious results as far as the success of the venture is concerned.

SELECTING THE TEAM LEADER

The selection of the team leader for a re-engineering project is clearly an important issue from the point of view of the effective functioning of the team and also in terms of the message that is conveyed to the rest of the organization. The latter should not be treated lightly since there is no doubt that a message will be both sent and received, whether positive or negative. Because of this the first criterion should be that the person selected should be someone who is, and is seen as, a high performer, rather than someone who has the time and can be spared. It is an interesting comment on humanity that those who are genuinely the busiest are often also those who are able, and usually willing, to take on more and to deliver the required output.

The second criterion should be the candidate's level of knowledge of the process in question. Ideal candidates are likely to be managers who are in charge of departments which are central to the processes under review. Some people would say that a knowledge of the process can be an impediment in the sense that it can get in the way and so limit our ability to explore all possible options. In our experience, however, as long as the other necessary attributes are present, this is not a serious concern, and there is no doubt that a detailed understanding of the present situation can be very beneficial.

The third criterion for selection concerns the personal qualities that the leader brings to the group. Some of these are self-evident, for example an active interest and enthusiasm, whereas others are less so. The effectiveness of groups is in no small way influenced by the balance of thinking modes and team roles that are contained within them, and so these should be taken into account. As far as the leader is concerned the ideal candidate is likely to be an 'ideas person', someone who has the ability to see beyond the present, without being limited by current constraints. There are, of course, other requirements for an effective team and these are covered in the section on team members, but given the radical nature of re-engineering projects the leaders of such teams should ideally have a high degree of imagination. However, if a candidate has all the other required qualities except the latter; the issue can, and must, be addressed in the selection of the team members so that the necessary balance of team roles is in place.

FACILITATOR

During the last few years the term facilitator has become more familiar but is often misunderstood and improperly applied. The origins of the role lie first in the recognition that the reason that groups so often underperform is much more to do with a lack of management of the way that they are working, in other words their 'process', than any lack of technical knowledge concerning the task at hand. A great deal is now known and understood about the way that groups operate and the complex dynamics that have a profound effect on their ability to succeed. This knowledge though is not widely enough shared among people who work in groups whether they are concerned with problem-solving, re-engineering or for that matter running the department or the organization. The result of this is that most groups perform nowhere near their potential which is both disappointing and wasteful.

There is no doubt that groups perform best in their task when they are managing the way they work, their process, but equally it is quite difficult during the early stages for one person to do both. It should be said that the ultimate objective should always be to equip people in the organization to be able to manage the dynamics of groups as they are working on the task, but this involves a fairly long-term development process. Because of this, and because re-engineering projects are both big and important, facilitators are used to observe the way that the groups are working and to ensure that nothing is happening in the dynamics of the meetings that is impairing the quality and the quantity of their output.

The second basis of the facilitator role is the recognition that groups perform best when they use an appropriate structure and defined techniques to help and guide them. Furthermore, for the most part people learn best from practical experience rather than abstract theory so the best time to provide training in the different techniques is when they are actually required. The facilitator, given the knowledge, is obviously in a good position to provide this.

In our experience providing groups with skilled facilitation is an absolute prerequisite if they are to perform to their full potential. This is particularly important with re-engineering projects because they are dealing with subjects that will have a material effect on the performance of the organization and because, by their nature, they are difficult to repeat if they fail the first time.

The role of the facilitator involves working mainly with the leader, but also with the team, to ensure that the project is successful. The main tasks that this entails are to prepare the meetings with the leader, to attend the meetings of the team, possibly to train the team in the different techniques that they will need and finally to review the team meetings with the leader.

Adequate preparation is required if the meetings are to be productive, and experience shows that the facilitator can be of great assistance to the leader in ensuring this. The preparation should include what the team will be trying to achieve in the next step and how they will approach the task. Preparation meetings generally take between half and one hour and the resulting plan should be written down and should include who will do what and estimated timings.

At the meeting itself the facilitator role is primarily to observe group process and to intervene and give guidance, through the leader, if the team seems to be going off track. It is not a prime responsibility of the facilitator to be engaged in the task itself. It may be that there is a requirement to train the team in a particular technique as a part of some of the meetings and where this is the case it can be performed by the leader, the facilitator, or the external consultant if one is being used. The ideal is that the team leader conducts such training sessions, but the level of knowledge that exists in the team and the training skills of the team leader may necessitate other arrangements.

Since BPR is a project-based rather than an ongoing activity it is of less importance than it otherwise would be that the leader conducts the training, but it is of absolute importance that the training is performed well and the techniques are applied correctly. It makes sense in an organization that intends to spread the use of BPR after the initial projects to ensure that their internal facilitators become knowledgeable and skilled in both the techniques themselves and the delivery of effective training sessions, and in these circumstances preference should be given to their development rather than the development of the leader's training skills.

After BPR project meetings the facilitator needs to discuss with the leader the meetings' task and process, to learn any lessons and to consider how to use them in making the next meeting even better. This session should take place immediately following the meeting, since the important issues will still be clearly in mind, and usually lasts for about 45 minutes.

SELECTING THE FACILITATOR

The nature and importance of the facilitator role make it particularly important that the appropriate people are selected. The first criterion should be that the facilitator should come from an area of the organization that is not a significant part of the process that is being re-engineered, because the role is concerned with the process of the work rather than the task itself. Since most of us are brought up to be very task oriented and prefer to get involved in this way, selecting people who have no particular knowledge of the process in question and who can therefore take a more disinterested view and concentrate on the 'how' rather than the 'what' is recommended.

The second criterion relates to the personal characteristics needed to be a successful facilitator. Since the people chosen have no conventional line authority over the leaders or indeed the teams they are working with, they need to be able to influence those that they are dealing with in a rather different way. Certainly they will need to be so-called 'people people' who enjoy working with others and who have a developmental rather than a directive style. They need to be bright and perceptive, able to think quickly and fluently with an ability to confront important issues in a way that does not alienate others or take the ownership of the project away from the leader and the team. At first glance it may seem a tall order to find people with these attributes but it is our experience that they do exist though usually in a raw and untrained form.

EXTERNAL CONSULTANT

The role of the external consultant is hotly debated. Some people see the role in a very positive light and so use consultants frequently, others treat them as a necessary evil and for yet others the whole idea of bringing outsiders in is anathema. It is not our purpose here to argue the relative merits of these views, rather to outline the different consultancy styles that exist, the potential roles that such people can play in BPR projects and, importantly, the guidelines for getting the best value for money from them. As consultants ourselves we do, of course, have a vested interest in this issue but we see so many examples of bad consultancy practice and so many organizations who deploy this resource inappropriately that we are not in the least surprised that the profession has such a bad name with some people.

There are three types of consultancy, 'expert', 'doctor/patient' and 'process' and most consultant organizations specialize in one or the other. For BPR projects the first and the third styles can be used, so these need to be explained in rather more detail. Expert consultants come into an organization and use their knowledge of a certain subject to tell the organization what it should do and, once accepted, to implement it. A process consultant on the other hand is one who draws the answers out of the people in the organization using a combination of training, development and facilitative skill, and who provides any necessary support as those involved go about the implementation. One clear difference between the two styles is that ownership rests with the expert consultant where one is used and with the organization in the case of the process consultant.

Process consultants work on the assumption that answers already exist within the minds of people in the organization and that it is a matter of accessing them. They also work with the belief that where the ownership resides is a key issue and that it must at all costs be with the organization rather than with the consultant since if this not the case it is likely that the particular programme, process or system will collapse once the consultant leaves.

In a general sense this logic is difficult to argue with but there are a number of additional factors that need to be taken into account concerning BPR. The first is that BPR is not natural development, rather it is radical and fundamental change that may, and probably will, take the organization into uncharted waters so there is a legitimate question that can be asked concerning whether the answers do exist in the organization at present.

The second consideration is an extension of the first and concerns the ability of people to 'see the wood for the trees'. Because many of those involved are likely to have been with the organization for some time, maybe for years, it is quite possible that they will have lost some of the ability to see past the 'trees' in their organization and to be able to think radically differently. This is in no way to disparage them for in our own circumstances we can all be affected in the same way.

The third issue is that whereas organizations and the processes they use are different, much can be learned from the experience of others when it comes to the actual process of re-engineering. Consultants will have this kind of knowledge if they have performed BPR assignments for other clients.

There is a potency about these matters, but we cannot discount the fundamental importance of the ownership being in the right place, which is with the organization. Our conclusion therefore is that the appropriate style for BPR is process consultancy with elements of expert consultancy used appropriately and with great skill and care such that the ownership remains in the correct place. The combination of skills that are needed to use this approach are quite rare.

The external consultant can bring a number of useful and legitimate ideas and skills to a BPR project but there are also one or two traps for the unwary client that unscrupulous consultants may be eager to exploit. First, the consultancy should show a full understanding of BPR and where it fits in the process of organization change and development.

Second, is a need for a clear and well-defined methodology that is openly described and discussed. Beware those who say that every case is different and that they develop the most appropriate method depending on the circumstances. This means they have no method and probably no experience either.

Third, the consultant should bring the ability to train internal people in the whole approach and also the specific tools and techniques that are needed to re-engineer a process thoroughly and effectively.

Fourth, since BPR has to be managed from the top while the projects themselves involve people from lower levels, there is an important role in ensuring effective liaison and communication between all those involved. Although this can be handled by internal resources, there is often a good case for using outside consultants as they can often see the requirement more clearly and should have the necessary range of skills to make sure that it is performed well.

CHOOSING THE CONSULTANCY

There are a number of consultancies that are competent in the field of BPR, but far fewer than those that claim expertise so caution is required. BPR projects are too big and too important to be put at risk by poor advice. The keys in selecting a consultancy are to be sure that it conforms to the outline discussed above and then to check the personal 'chemistry' between the consultant and those in the organization who will be involved in the project – particularly important since any one project will last for a number of months at least. Remember as well that the consultancy salesperson will not necessarily be the operating consultant.

CO-ORDINATOR

In larger organizations where more than one project is under way at the same time there will be a need for a co-ordinator. In smaller organizations and when there is only one project this role can sometimes be added to the facilitator's responsibility. Certainly it must not be forgotten.

The co-ordinator is responsible first for 'oiling the wheels' of the entire project and making sure that the necessary backup and support is given to the teams. Second, the role involves ensuring that there is sufficient cross-referencing between the different BPR projects. Sometimes parts of different processes are common and where this is the case there is a need to ensure that there is no unnecessary duplication of effort and that the conclusions reached by different teams are compatible. Third, the co-ordinator should ensure that potentially useful information is stored for use by future teams or others in the organization. This may include anything from training modules to lessons learned from putting the methodology into practice in this particular environment.

CHOOSING THE CO-ORDINATOR

The co-ordinator role is a part-time one. It requires good administrative ability and enough understanding of the organization and its goals to be able to identify important issues between the teams. There is no particular requirement for the co-ordinator to be a senior person, though in many situations this is what happens on the basis that it is an indication of the commitment of the organization.

A way of dealing with this that does not use too much management time is to give the responsibility to a senior person, usually a director, who has access to existing support either with a secretary or a personal assistant.

TEAM MEMBERS

BPR projects are undertaken by specially selected teams of employees and the members need to be chosen with care. The members of the team receive guidance and support from the consultant and from the internal facilitator and it is their collective responsibility with the leader to use the methodology and re-engineer the particular process under review. This happens largely during the regular meetings of the group though it is normal for there to be a requirement for various actions in the interim. The meetings are usually of half a day's duration and take place every two weeks throughout the project which will certainly be a number of months and could be over a year depending on the scale and complexity of the process being re-engineered.

SELECTING THE TEAM MEMBERS

There are a number of aspects of selection that should be taken into account and the first concerns level of seniority. Re-engineering teams usually comprise people from different levels of the organization. Middle-level people who are involved in the process will usually be appropriate for the task since they should have enough of a grasp of the detail while also being able to see the entire picture. Where possible, however, members of the team should not have a direct reporting relationship with each other. It is also wise to ensure that the group contains some members who are outside the process and who can bring in useful knowledge and skills. Obvious examples of this would be an IT expert and a Human Resources specialist.

Generally speaking the team should consist of between five and seven people, with seven being ideal, including the leader but excluding the facilitator, since this has been demonstrated to be the optimum size to tackle such work.

When selecting it is also necessary to balance the members in terms of team roles. Each of us when working in groups have natural strengths and preferences as far as the roles we play in the working of the team. Research has indicated conclusively that 'unbalanced' teams do not work as well as balanced ones. For example Belbin, who is one of the primary researchers in this area, found that groups consisting exclusively of the most apparently intelligent and able people always performed badly when compared with other groups which contained a membership that was more balanced in the team roles.[1]

His research findings have been demonstrated to be true on countless occasions in our own experience, let alone that of others, and should be taken into account in the selection of team members for any BPR project. These projects are designed to have a radical impact on the functioning of the organization and so must be taken very seriously.

The well-balanced team will consist of people who fulfil the following roles which are illustrated with typical behaviour statements to assist in the identification of potential candidates:

- *Chairperson*
  'What we are here to do is ...'
  'Let's do this first and then move on to that.'
  'To summarize, the main points seem to be ...'
  'Let's get back to the main issue ...'
- *Shaper*
  'What we have to do is ...'
  'We're wasting time, we should ...'
  'No, you're wrong, the main issue is ...'
  'If we put what you have said with the other suggestions we can ...'
- *Plant*
  'What about ...?'

'Turning that on its head gives us ...'
'A good idea would be ...'
'Let's look at that from a different angle.'
- *Monitor/evaluator*
  'We have to watch out for ...'
  'Let's not overlook ...'
  'The problem with this is ...'
  'This is telling us that we should ...'
- *Company worker*
  'Let's get this up on the flip chart.'
  'We could do that within our budget.'
  'Given the time we've got we could ...'
  'If we do that we would be getting nearer to the result.'
- *Resource investigator*
  'What a great idea.'
  'I know someone who can.'
  'Don't worry, I can get them.'
  'I can talk to them and put our point of view.'
- *Team worker*
  'There's no need to fight about it.'
  'Let's listen to Sally's idea.'
  'Why don't you explain that a little bit more.'
  'Let's build on Fred's idea.'
- *Completer/Finisher*
  'You can't do that, we'll be a week late.'
  'Let me check that.'
  'What about article 3 in sub-paragraph iv of the second volume?'
  'What we have to do if the whole thing is going to work is ...'

Time will be well spent taking care in the selection of team members using these guidelines and for anyone interested there is a simple questionnaire-based exercise that is readily available to assist in the identification of peoples' team role preferences.

THE RESOURCING REQUIREMENTS FOR BPR PROJECTS

As well as the roles there are two main resourcing implications of starting a BPR project. In part these are identifiable before the project begins, but there are others that, of necessity, are less definable at the outset. Training is the first and most predictable requirement. It goes without saying that organizations which do not provide people with the tools to do the job are very unlikely to reap the benefit of re-engineering; the only questions concern who to train, how much training to give and in what context to provide it, for example through training programmes ahead of time or during the course of the re-engineering project itself.

There are different ways of handling this requirement and thought needs to be given to the method that best fits the organization and its situation. Assuming that the senior team has been through a workshop on the subject prior to committing itself to the approach and so understands enough about the technique and its implications, the main training that is needed concerns the facilitator, the leader and the members of the team. The decisions made may also be influenced by whether or not external consultants are being used to assist with the project since if they are it is assumed that they will be on hand to provide the necessary inputs. For the purpose of this part of the discussion we have assumed that either the latter will be the case or that there is a skilled and knowledgeable enough internal resource that can fulfil the same function.

Expert facilitation is an essential ingredient in the success of a BPR project. This requires both generic facilitator skills and also a knowledge of the tools and techniques that will be used by the team in progressing the work. The techniques that will be required include those that are described elsewhere in this book and a range of more conventional problem-solving tools including brainstorming, fishbone diagrams, the six-word diagram, force field analysis and the modified Delphi. We find that basic facilitator skills can be taught during a five-day programme and that this provides a solid foundation for those who will be involved in this role.

Leaders of BPR teams also need to be trained before they start their projects if they are to fulfil their role successfully. It is not satisfactory for them to be put in a position of being only 'one page ahead' of the members of the team. Our approach involves them in a three-day implementation workshop where we teach the overall methodology and also give people practice in the tools that they will be using during the project.

As far as members of the team are concerned our experience indicates, for the most part, that the best time to provide training in the techniques is during the meetings themselves and at the time when they need them. This is because there is clear evidence that people learn best from experience and that they find it quite difficult to translate lessons learned in the classroom into practice. The use of the techniques in a BPR project is too important to risk this happening.

The other main resource that is often required concerns IT. BPR usually, though not always, involves making more use of new developments in this field some of which provide opportunities that are quite staggering in their potential and in their impact. The difficulty, however, is that it is not possible to predict what the requirement will be. Ready-made software may be available to meet the needs of the new process but on the other hand it may be necessary to design software to fit the particular purpose. The senior team must consider this at the outset since there is little point in re-engineering a process and then deciding that the organization cannot, or will not, afford the investment required to put it into practice. It is better that, if there are limits, they are defined at the outset and built into the brief given to the team.

A number of important roles and resources have a legitimate part to play in BPR projects and organizations which do not provide them, suitably prepared, trained and supported stand very little chance of achieving the gains that are possible and can cause serious damage to their health and operating performance.

Notes

1. Belbin, M.J. (1981), *Management Teams, Why They Succeed or Fail*, Oxford: Heinemann.

6 Structuring Business Process Re-engineering

Before specific individuals can be appointed to the roles outlined in the previous chapter, there are two immediate needs: first to define the key processes that exist within the organization, then to select those that will be re-engineered. Although these may sound like relatively straightforward tasks, they can be quite difficult and there are a number of pitfalls that can trap the unsuspecting organization.

These two tasks should normally be carried out by senior teams within the organization. If re-engineering is to take place across the whole organization, then normally the Executive Team should be given this job. If re-engineering is to be carried out within a business unit or specific division, then it makes sense for the senior team at this level to be involved. In general, the job of defining and selecting processes should be carried out by the team that oversees that part of the business.

Teams often find it difficult to define their key processes, usually because they are used to thinking in terms of the specific tasks that go to make up a process and the departments that are responsible for managing those tasks. Hence when a team is asked to identify its main business processes it will tend to suggest functions like 'training' or 'sales' or 'production'. As we shall see, these are not genuine processes and are unlikely to be suitable candidates for re-engineering.

Another problem is that it is not always clear how general or how detailed a process description should be. At one end of the scale, typing a letter is a process. At the other end of this scale, fulfilling a sales order is a process that may include major activities such as new product design or distribution. Within these two extremes a decision has to be made as to what to include and the level of detail required.

A third difficulty is deciding which processes should be re-engineered. We know of some organizations where business process re-engineering has been carried out on virtually any process that has been identified. Usually in these cases it is not genuine process re-engineering but a modified form of problem-solving that the organization has been introducing. At one well-known High Street service organization we were told that all the branches were re-engineering their processes. A senior manager confided that the exercise had been a nightmare for the staff involved. Branches were 'trained' by the internal consultants in how to identify processes and then improve them. Lists of processes running into the hundreds were identified within each branch. Clearly this level of breadth and detail is likely to render the exercise a failure right from the start.

In our experience these decisions should be carried out in a carefully structured way that reflects the strategic importance attached to this task and are best made by the senior team using a workshop format to define and select their processes for re-engineering. This is called a Process Quality Management (PQM) workshop and it was originally designed to enable Executive Teams to manage and improve their key business processes. Over the years we have adapted PQM's original format to incorporate the latest thinking in BPR and to bring our own experiences of facilitating this kind of workshop to bear on improving its format.

The workshop is normally held over two days, and should adopt the following format:

Day 1
Agree ground rules.
Establish the mission.
Develop and agree critical success factors (CSFs).
Develop key business processes (KBPs)

Day 2
Agree key business processes.
Map KBPs on to CSFs.
Prioritize processes.
Select processes for re-engineering.

At the outset of the workshop the team should agree a set of ground rules to which it will adhere. Although this is normally good practice for most types of meetings or workshops, it is particularly important for this workshop because the team will be making some critical and strategic decisions that will influence profoundly the future direction of the re-engineering effort and, ultimately, the organization itself. Therefore these decisions must be made effectively and on the basis of real consensus rather than just a simple majority. Typical ground rules for this type of workshop are:

- Avoid arguing narrowly for the interests of your own department.
- Base arguments and decisions on facts rather than opinions.
- Don't just 'go along with the rest of the group' when you disagree.

- Voice any concerns you may have.
- Make use of the devil's advocate role.
- Listen, don't just wait to speak.
- All decisions to be made by full consensus.

Making decisions by consensus requires some skill, and usually the active intervention of a facilitator to ensure that the majority view does not force itself through. Some of the guidelines that we have found helpful in assisting teams on the technique of consensus decision-making are as follows:

- Avoid arguing for your own individual judgements. Approach the task on the basis of logic.
- Avoid changing your mind purely to reach agreement and avoid conflict. Support only those decisions with which you can agree with at least in part.
- Avoid conflict-reducing techniques such as voting, averaging, or trading when reaching decisions.
- View differences of opinion as helpful rather than as hindrances in making decisions.
- Be prepared to consider agreeing with decisions once you feel all of your important concerns have been discussed.

Once the team has agreed how decisions will be made, and the behaviours required by individuals to support this, the next step in the PQM format is to define and agree the mission of the whole organization. These days most organizations have a mission statement, and if so the team can start with this. However, if this workshop is being held at a lower level or for a separate division of the organization, then it should establish its own local mission statement if it does not have one.

Starting the workshop with a statement of the organization's mission is important since it ensures that everything that follows is driven and guided by the purpose of the organization. The mission statement provides a touchstone against which the team can validate its decisions, or help it choose between competing alternatives.

If a local mission is required then it is important that this is established without too much debate and wrangling. Although this debate may be healthy for an organization establishing its mission, this task should not be allowed to detract from the main aim of the PQM workshop, which is to define and select processes for re-engineering. A skilled facilitator can help the team establish a workable mission statement in the space of two to three hours. This can be refined over time, and the views of others sought to improve it and ensure that it has widespread appeal and credibility. For the purposes of this workshop, however, the team must have some form of mission statement that will guide the main activities and decisions to follow.

The mission statement, whether new or existing, should be assessed against strict criteria. Sometimes mission statements are little more than a grand set of words, full of what is commonly referred to as 'motherhood' and 'apple pie'. If this is the case then it will serve little useful purpose. To be useful and practical, a mission statement should be:

- understandable
- communicable
- believable
- usable

The team should evaluate its mission statement against these criteria, and agree whatever changes are necessary to ensure that it meets them. If the existing statement is a grand but meaningless set of words, it will probably be sensible for the team to develop and adapt a new statement for the workshop, and later work on the task of combining this with the existing version or even replacing it completely.

The second step in this workshop is for the team to agree a small number of sub-goals that follow directly from the goal stated within the mission. These are the factors that are critical to the success of the organization, as defined by its mission statement. They refer to the 'what' rather than the 'how' of the business, and are normally called critical success factors (CSFs). Once again this can be a difficult exercise. One of the main problems is keeping down the number of CSFs that are likely contenders for this title. We recommend that no more than eight should be agreed by the team. This is partly because it becomes very difficult to work with a larger number. But it is also an effective way of determining the 'criticality' of these success factors. If there are more than eight there is a reasonable chance that some are important but not critical.

Reducing the number to eight is a useful exercise, since it forces the senior team to agree what is critical to its success. Keeping to eight CSFs tends to exclude those sub-goals that are more important to the empires or egos of individuals, and enables the team to concentrate on what is genuinely important.

The team should start the process of generating CSFs by holding a brainstorming session in which it generates one-word descriptions of all the things that could have an impact (positive or negative) on achieving the mission. Once this has been completed, and using the entire list that has been generated, the team should identify those factors that are critical to achieving the mission. It should avoid suggesting potential solutions ('a new computerised system') or things that reflect *how* it operates rather than *what* it wants to achieve (for example, 'develop new products'). As a rule of thumb, the words 'we must have ...' should be capable of preceding any genuine CSF. Potential solutions should be used to identify the true goal by asking: 'What would this help us to achieve?'

In narrowing the list of CSFs to no more than eight, the result should reflect the key parts of the business and its links with other organizations. We would normally expect to find CSFs relating to suppliers, customers, staff, environmental factors, systems, and equipment. This list of broad areas can be used to assess the CSFs produced by the team to ensure they have not omitted a key part of their business.

These CSFs should therefore refer to the main sub-goals of the organization. To be genuinely critical, it should not be possible for the mission to be achieved without each individual sub-goal. If all of the sub-goals are achieved, then it should follow that the organization will be successful in its mission. Thus each CSF should be necessary to the mission, and collectively they should be sufficient to achieve the mission. This necessary and sufficient rule should be applied to each CSF individually, and to the final list collectively. Once the team is satisfied that it has defined its final list it is ready to move on to the third step of the workshop, that of defining its key business processes.

Although defining key business processes is the primary task of the workshop, the team must not consider it until this stage in the proceedings. By first defining its mission and critical success factors, the team will be able to ensure that its main processes are actually serving to achieve those goals. All too often the processes and activities within an organization have little to do with what it is aiming to achieve, and this approach helps the team get back to the basic reasons for the organization's existence.

This is a critical stage of the workshop and it is important that the team defines genuine processes since this will affect the subsequent work of the re-engineering team. Sometimes teams find it difficult to see sets of apparently distinct activities carried out in different parts of the company as part of one single process. For example, the installation of computer equipment by technical experts may not be seen as related to the activities of those involved in the storage of goods within the warehouse, yet both may be parts of the process of procurement.

Although this may sound fairly obvious, it is surprising how often teams and individuals fall into the trap of defining their processes too narrowly. On numerous occasions when we have been asked to advise teams struggling to improve or re-engineer a process we have found that the difficulty lies in the team having defined the process too narrowly. The breakthrough comes when we suggest that those processes and departments seen as lying outside the process under review, and thus outside the scope for change, are in fact part of the process and that its boundaries should be expanded to include these. More often than not, the original boundaries coincided with departmental and functional boundaries, illustrating the difficulty people have seeing activities performed in different parts of the company as part of an entire process.

In defining the organization's key business processes, the senior team needs to avoid this and several other potential traps. Teams sometimes find it useful to begin each process description with a verb, since this ensures that it is concentrating on activities not outcomes. Any process should have a beginning, middle and end, and these must be capable of being identified for each process that the team has suggested. All processes should be capable of being measured and managed, although verbs like 'measure' or 'manage' should be excluded from process descriptions. 'Measure customer satisfaction' is not a genuine process, but rather the activity of measuring the outcome of a process; it is the process the team needs to define. Similarly, 'manage stock control' is not a process but the activity involved in managing part of a process; again it is the process the team should identify.

A useful distinction here is that between operational processes and support processes. An organization's operational processes will be those sets of activities that directly produce its key 'outputs' and which are received by its external customers. In manufacturing organizations these will be those processes directly involved in the production of a product. In service organizations they will be those processes leading directly to the provision of services. On the other hand, support processes will be those processes where the final output is received by others within the organization. These will most likely be administrative processes, covering areas such as finance, management activities, or staff training. In this workshop, the team should aim to define a combination of operational and support processes. Although all operational processes should be part of the final list produced by the team, some care will be needed to distinguish between those support processes that are genuinely critical parts of the business, and those that are less important. Ultimately this will be a matter of judgement for the team involved, though it needs to be aware of the danger of including too many processes in its final list. In our experience a final list of about 15 processes ensures the right level of detail and breadth.

Since this list of processes will be used to guide the subsequent re-engineering projects each process should be properly defined and the whole list ought to represent all the main activities within the organization. The processes should be genuinely cross-functional and be high-level processes rather than detailed activities. Although the principles of re-engineering can be applied to lower-level processes, the gains are

Critical success factors Business processes	Lowest delivery cost for comparable models	High levels of customer satisfaction	Excellent suppliers	Excellent dealers	Highest product quality in automotive industry	Highly skilled and motivated employees	New products that satisfy market needs	Opportunities for new business	Number of CSFs	Performance
P1 Educate suppliers			x				x	x	4	E
P2 Train employees	x	x		x	x	x	x	x	7	B
P3 Monitor competitors	x	x	x	x	x		x	x	7	D
P4 Select and certify suppliers	x		x		x		x	x	5	E
P5 Select and certify dealers		x		x		x		x	4	C
P6 Educate dealers		x		x		x		x	4	C
P7 Support automobiles sold	x	x		x	x			x	5	B
P8 Specify requirements for new products		x	x				x	x	4	C
P9 Develop new products	x	x	x	x	x		x	x	7	B
P10 Advertise products		x				x		x	3	A
P11 Research the market-place	x	x						x	3	D
P12 Process dealer orders		x		x					3	B
P13 Monitor customer/dealer complaints		x		x	x		x		4	D
P14 Develop customer/dealer satisfaction		x			x		x	x	4	D
P15 Develop product quality	x		x		x		x	x	5	B
P16 Define future skill needs				x		x	x	x	4	D
P17 Market/push the company		x		x		x	x	x	4	B
P18 Get consensus of manufacturing design	x		x		x		x	x	5	E
P19 Monitor purchasers' automotive needs		x		x	x	x	x	x	5	E
P20 Announce new products		x					x	x	3	B

Table 6.1 A list of processes

likely to be much greater when dealing with processes that span several departments and functions of the organization. Detailed descriptions of each process are not necessary at this point, and one of the early tasks of the re-engineering team will be to improve the definition of a process and its boundaries. We will describe how this should be done in a later chapter. In general, the use of an experienced facilitator will help ensure that at this stage the processes that have been defined by the team meet the criteria outlined above and are sufficient to enable the most to be obtained from the re-engineering teams who have the task of working with these processes.

An illustrative list of processes is shown in Table 6.1. The example is taken from the motor industry, and shows the main processes that exist within a motor vehicle manufacturer. Once the team has agreed its final list of processes it should set them out in matrix like that in Table 6.1, which also contains the critical success factors. In this way it is easy to compare the main activities in the organization with its main goals.

Using this matrix, the relationship between processes and critical success factors can be defined. The team does this by taking each CSF in turn and asking: 'What processes have to be performed especially well if we are to achieve this CSF?' Each process that fulfils this criterion is marked by a cross in the box under the relevant CSF. The team should then review all the processes that have been marked as contributing to the successful achievement of a CSF and ask if, taken together, they are sufficient to its achievement. This will highlight if there are any gaps in the list of processes; these gaps may be due to some processes having not been enumerated, and if so they can be added now. More significantly, it will highlight if there are any new processes that the organization needs to start performing. For example, a food distribution company did not have any process for training and developing its staff. As is often the case it had started as a small company where this function was not deemed necessary, and had grown into a much larger one without considering the need to add a proper HR department. During its PQM workshop the senior team had identified 'highly skilled staff' as a critical success factor, and then came to the belated recognition during this phase of the workshop that it did nothing to enhance or maintain staff skill levels.

Having performed this step for each CSF, the team should then consider each process and count the number of CSFs it contributes to (indicated by marked boxes), and write this number in the penultimate column. Occasionally this can reveal some processes that do not impact on any CSFs. This is the converse of the situation facing the food distributor, and highlights activities that may have been relevant in years gone by, but which are no longer critical to the performance of the company.

Yet owing to a combination of tradition and a failure to question the true relevance of activities, these processes remain intact. If this is the case, the team needs to consider whether it needs to maintain this process or whether the time has come for its demise.

The number of CSFs that any process impacts gives an approximate and relative measure of its importance. Processes that affect a large number of CSFs are likely to be more critical to the performance of the organization than those that impact only one or two. Hence the matrix provides a useful and practical measure of process importance that can be used when selecting processes for re-engineering. We will discuss this shortly. However, before this is done, the next step in the workshop involves rating the performance of each process. Taking each in turn, the team should agree a rating on the following five-point scale:

A = Excellent performance
B = Good performance
C = Fair performance
D = Inadequate performance
E = Poor performance

Rating performance can be a difficult task, since objective data may not be available to make accurate judgements on the performance of each process. A more common difficulty, however, is that individual members of the team will feel bound to defend the performance of processes that come under their remit. If this is the case, the team should remind itself of its ground rules and the need to avoid defensiveness. If the processes are truly cross-functional any single individual will not feel wholly responsible for a process, and the leader of the team (chief executive or managing director) should emphasize that the purpose of this part of the workshop is not to criticize individuals but to make an objective appraisal of parts of the business, recognizing that many external factors may contribute to this.

Having completed the matrix, the team is ready to move on to the fourth step in the workshop, which involves selecting those processes that will be re-engineered. There are at least four criteria that can be used to guide the selections: the strategic importance of the process, its current 'health', customer expectations, and opportunity.

The strategic importance of the process is perhaps the most obvious criterion. By re-engineering processes that are central to its overall strategy an organization can greatly enhance its ability to fulfil that strategy. For example, a hospital that has a three-year strategy of increasing the number of operations it performs by 20 per cent in a climate where demand and resources are likely to remain static will need to consider its surgical intervention process for radical change if it is to achieve this target. As stated above, an approximate but practical measure of the relative strategic importance of each process is indicated by the number of CSFs each process impacts upon, as shown in Table 6.1.

The health of an existing process, as indicated by the team's rating on a scale from A to E, can also influence selection decisions. Processes that are performing poorly can sometimes only be improved by a radical overhaul of the main steps and procedures involved. However, the usual response is to patch up the problem rather than change the process. Unfortunately, this usually involves introducing extra steps, checks and people into the process. Under these conditions a vicious circle is created as over time processes become top-heavy with a bureaucracy that increases the delays and errors that prompted its development in the first place. Such processes are ripe for re-engineering, and the benefits are likely to be immediately obvious.

A third criterion is the expectations of customers of the processes. These customers can be internal or external to the organization concerned, although the latter is more likely to be the case since the need for change is usually more obvious to those who are not part of the organization. A good example of this comes from one manufacturer in the textiles industry. The lead time of one of its manufacturing processes was 44 days, and for many years there was little internal or external pressure to change this. It was only when a main customer said it had found another supplier who could meet orders more quickly that the company decided a change was necessary. What is interesting in this case is that the manufacturer set two teams on the task of reducing the lead time. The first was given the instruction of taking out unnecessary steps and people in the process and reducing the lead time to an acceptable duration. The second team was set up by one of the directors who had recently attended a conference on Business Process Re-engineering. He asked this team to 'throw away the rule book' and design a completely new process without being constrained by the norms, unwritten rules and regulations that tended to influence how work was carried out within the company.

Both teams duly reported back their designs for the process. The first was able to reduce the lead time to 32 days by removing much of the 'fat' that had built up in the process over the years. In contrast, the re-engineering team had designed a radically new process that could achieve the same output in just 21 days. However, the changes required to do this were so fundamental and affected other parts of the company to such an extent that although the design was bold and provocative, it was seen as having little practical value.

The company returned to its customer with the good news that it now

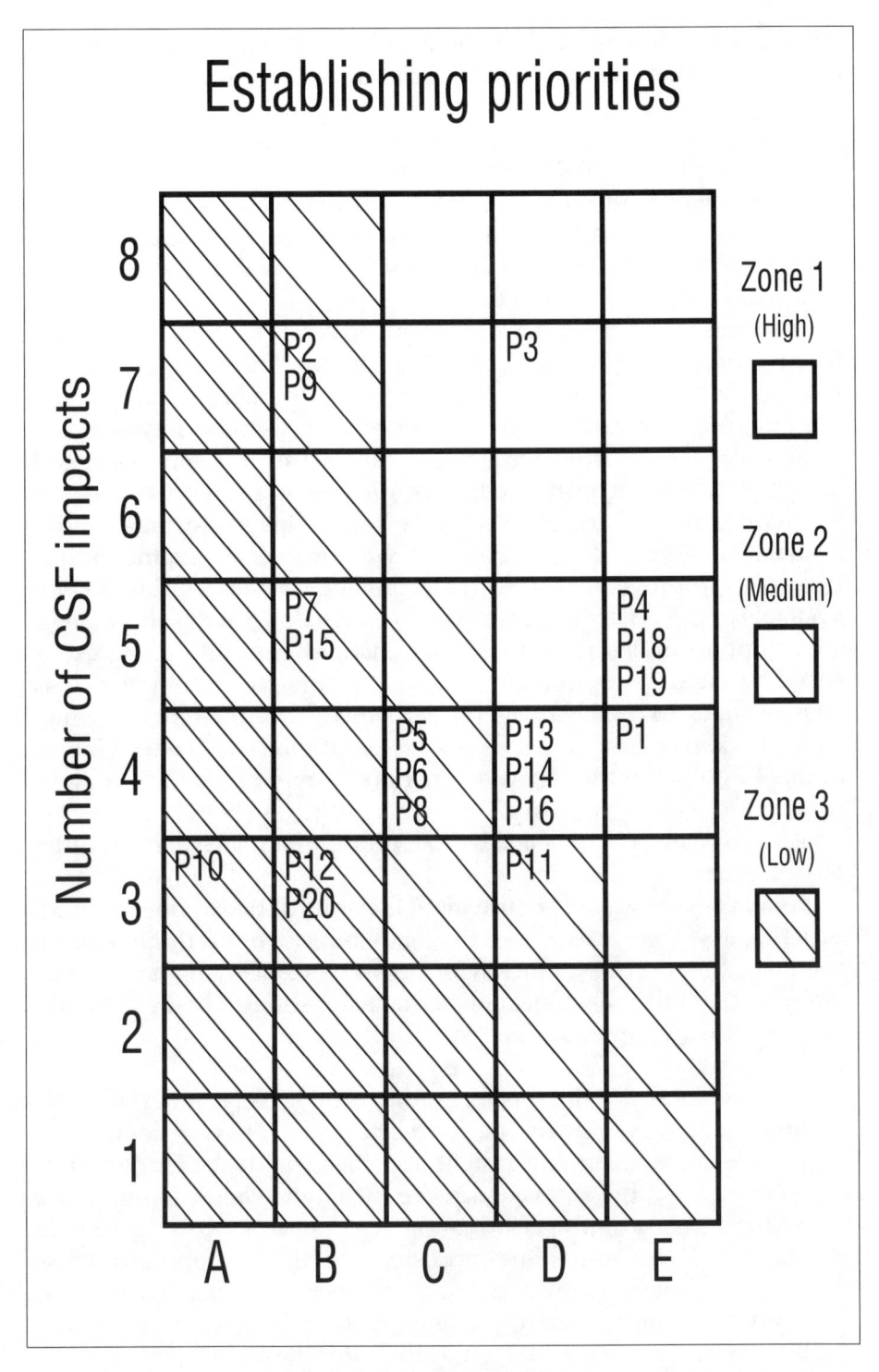

Figure 6.1 Prioritizing processes

could meet orders in 32 days, only to be told that this was not good enough since the customer had found an alternative supplier who could do it in nine! The company returned to its drawing board, and the re-engineering team was instructed to challenge and reject even the most basic assumptions it had made in its first effort: it had to get the process down to fewer than nine days. Although the design stage took much longer this time, a lead time of just four days was eventually achieved. At this point the company realized that it had just completed its first genuine re-engineering exercise.

In this case the expectations and demands of a customer had been the driving force behind the selection of the process for re-engineering and, indeed, the outcome to be achieved. A fourth criterion that could be used to select a process for re-engineering is the opportunity that exists to achieve desired outcomes. There can be several sources of such opportunity, and the team needs to adopt a broad perspective if it is not to overlook these during the selection stage. One source might be the availability of new technology. Often we don't recognize the need for change or improvement until the technology to enable this becomes available and we ask ourselves, 'what can we do with this technology?' Other opportunities may arise from changes currently being experienced by the organization concerned. A merger, for example, necessitates the need to establish one process where two different ones might have previously existed. Although the temptation may be to bring one of these into line with the other, the opportunity exists for a complete redesign. Whatever the source, an executive team should not overlook unusual or new circumstances that prompt the selection of certain processes for re-engineering.

It is, of course, possible to use more than one of these criteria. By constructing a second matrix, like that shown in Figure 6.1, the team can combine strategic importance with performance. Having entered each process number in the relevant box, the team should divide the matrix into the following three zones:

- Zone 1: These are the processes most strategically important to the organization yet their performance is relatively poor. These processes and their constituent activities should be chosen for re-engineering if the aim is to achieve high, quick and positive impact on the organization's performance.
- Zone 2: These important processes contain less opportunity for impact on the organization's performance, but once resources are freed from improving or re-engineering Zone 1 processes their improvement will add significantly to the achievement of the mission.

- Zone 3: These processes have minimum impact on the organization's performance, or are already currently performing highly and leave less room for improvement. They should be monitored to ensure they continue to perform well and should be improved after Zone 1 and Zone 2 processes have been given full attention.

The team should collectively discuss and agree where the boundaries for each of these three zones should fall. Having done this it will be able to select a small group of processes for re-engineering that will reflect their strategic importance to the organization and also their current performance and opportunity for improvement. The next stage in the re-engineering process is for specific teams to be appointed to take the processes that have been selected by the senior team during this workshop, and to begin the task of re-engineering them. We now turn to this task.

7 Understanding the Process

The first task for the re-engineering team is to obtain a clear and comprehensive understanding of the process that is to be re-engineered. Many authors on the subject have stated that business process re-engineering requires a 'blank page'. By this they mean that the new process should be designed as if from scratch, untainted by any of the assumptions, traditions and customs that may have led the process to its current state. While we would agree that the new process should not be influenced by features of the old, in our experience it is far more practical to start with a clear understanding of what is currently the case rather than an actual blank page. We know of several re-engineering teams that have attempted the latter, only to find themselves unable to make any progress because of disagreements about what they should be aiming for. By examining the current process in detail, charting its stages, and identifying its customers and their requirements, a re-engineering team is much more able to think creatively about what a new process should look like than if none of this existing knowledge is known.

Another reason why this first step is important is that it helps to create a truly process-oriented perspective among those in the team. Up until this time no one within the organization will have considered in detail the whole process. Individuals and departments corresponding to the main steps in the process will know their own roles, but few if any will have taken a broad view of the process in its entirety. A striking example of this came from an NHS Trust hospital with whom we worked. A small team had been established to examine the process by which surgical instruments were used, sterilized, and returned for use again. The team included surgeons, theatre nurses, porters, and sterilization technicians. Each was part of a separate department that was physically as well as functionally distinct from the others. It was little wonder that no one really knew what happened to the instruments outside their own area. One of the team's first tasks was to develop a flow chart for each of the four functional stages of the process. Next, each of the four flow charts were joined together, like a jigsaw, to show the whole picture.

75

Remarkably, though perhaps not surprisingly, this was the first time the process had been viewed and comprehended in its entirety. The team was able to see where problems occurred, and suggest how the process should be re-engineered.

We will describe the techniques that should be used to map a process in the next chapter. Here we will deal with the initial tasks of defining, and measuring the process to be re-engineered. Taken together, these tasks will assist the team to design a truly new process that is driven by customer requirements rather than historical antecedents, while at the same time avoiding the difficulty of doing this from a 'blank page'.

PROCESS BOUNDARIES

Initially the team should define the process and its boundaries. Although the executive team will have already identified and named the process, it is unlikely that they will have done this with the level of detail and rigour that is now required. The members of the re-engineering team will also benefit from developing a shared understanding of the process, since it is unlikely they will have been involved in the Process Quality Management workshop.

The boundaries of the process refer to the points where this process begins and ends, and where other processes lie in relation to it. Most organizations today consist of a complex array of processes and sub-processes. Although experts may talk of business processes as though they are there for everyone concerned to see, it is often a matter of judgement as to what is included as a sub-process and what is excluded as a separate process.

We can see this if we take a domestic process, like going on an overseas holiday. Where does this process begin? At the airport, or maybe at the travel agent six months earlier? Is the process of buying summer beach clothes a separate process or a sub-process of this one? And when does the process end: arriving at home two weeks later, or making the final payment on the credit card bill six months later and a few weeks before booking the following year's holiday?

A common mistake that re-engineering teams make is defining the process too narrowly. Because we are not used to taking a truly process-oriented view of work, we tend to see processes that exist within departments more easily than we see those that extend across departmental boundaries. The result is that important stages are often defined as lying outside the scope of the re-engineering team because they occur in other parts of the business. A process must be defined broadly and encompass other departments, since many of the gains come from resolving the difficulties that occur at the handover of work across departments.

Having defined the beginning and end of the process, the team should define the upper and lower boundaries. The upper boundary can be thought of as the point at which outputs from other processes enter the process under question. To return to the example of a holiday, the team may decide that shopping for clothes is a separate process, the output of which enters the process of going on holiday. Or it may decide that this should fall within the boundaries of the process, but that other activities, such as going to work, fall outside the process but produce an output (money) that is required by the process.

The lower boundary is the point at which outputs leave the process, to be used as inputs for other processes. Once again this will force the team to define what lies within the process under study and what is to be excluded. In the holiday example, photographic negatives may be defined as an output that leaves the process and is used as an input to a separate process of developing holiday snaps, or this may be defined as an important part of the whole process.

The boundaries of a process are the point at which inputs and outputs enter and leave the process. Having defined these boundaries, the team should list the inputs and outputs to complete the picture. It is useful to distinguish between primary inputs (those that are required at the beginning of the process) and secondary inputs (those that enter the process through the upper boundary). A similar distinction should be drawn between primary and secondary outputs. The latter can be thought of as 'by-products' of the process. They are produced by steps in the process but are not its *raison d'être*. In contrast, the primary outputs of a process are those that the process exists to produce and which are received by its main customers.

The final task in this stage of defining the process boundaries is to determine the customers and suppliers of the process. The re-engineering team should have a clear knowledge of who these are and their requirements. Teams often find it difficult to agree on the customer of a process, since it is not always clear who this is. For example, a team examining the process of producing a dairy product may see the distribution department, or the supermarket that receives and then sells the product or the person that buys it as the main customer. Since the introduction of an internal market-place in health care the question of who is the customer has brought attention on purchasing authorities, budget holders within hospitals, and fundholding GPs, as well as the patient.

These ambiguities are easily resolved if we allow distinctions between different types of customers, rather than trying to apply the label to only one party. In fact there can be up to five different types of customers of a process, as previously shown in Figure 2.1, and the re-engineering team should define who falls into which category. The primary customer is the party that receives the primary output from the process, which will have been defined when the boundaries of the process were being agreed. Secondary customers receive the secondary outputs also defined during that stage. Indirect customers are those that are next in line after the primary customer. Although they will not directly receive the output from the process, they will be affected by late deliveries or errors in the product or service that constitutes the primary output. With many processes, the primary, secondary and indirect customers will be internal to the organization. External customers can be one of two types: consumers and non-consumers. The latter includes distribution agents, such as supermarkets or retail branches, while the consumer is otherwise known as 'Joe Public'.

Determining the boundaries of the process to be re-engineered and its inputs, outputs, and customers is not easy and the re-engineering team will need to be patient and rigorous as it works towards this goal. However, the benefits of doing this often make themselves clear once the team becomes embroiled in the task of designing a new process. We have noted on several occasions that teams that stumble when they reach this stage often do so because they have not agreed on what falls within their remit and what falls outside it.

CUSTOMER REQUIREMENTS

The next step for the re-engineering team is to agree the requirements of these customers. Once again this is an important yet sometimes overlooked stage in the work of a re-engineering team. It is surprising how many teams attempt to create a new process without a clear understanding of its customer's requirements. Not only must the new process meet these requirements, but this stage also provides a valuable insight into what the team should be aiming for, and helps guide actions and improvements.

The process of negotiating requirements with internal customers is one that is rarely performed in most organizations, and many people will have little experience of doing this in a rigorous way. Most of the time these requirements are assumed, and little attempt is made to discover if they are valid even though many years may have passed since they were discussed with the customer. In a workshop we recently conducted within a large service organization, departments were asked to list and prioritize the requirements of their internal customers, while their customers were asked to list and prioritize their requirements of these departments. We then brought the groups together to share their lists. The differences were remarkable. Services that departments thought were important to their customers were deemed to be of little value by those customers, while others that *were* important to them appeared low on the lists of the departments. People within the groups said to each other: 'We had no idea that was important to you, we thought it made little difference.'

Representatives from the re-engineering team need to arrange and hold meetings with the primary customers of the process in order to agree their requirements. At these meetings, every attempt should be made to challenge the *status quo* and explore alternatives to the current situation. Questions to ask of the customer are: why is this needed? Is all of it required? Could some of the tasks be better performed by your department? The aim is to question rigorously some of the assumptions that are currently determining the work that is done within the process to produce the output, and to arrive at an understanding of the customer's real requirements.

In doing this we have found the technique of 'logical levelling' to be very helpful. This technique is derived from Neuro-Linguistic Programming, and is based on the fact that there are different levels of abstractness in the language we use. We may talk of a hamburger, or at a more abstract level we may talk of fast food. An even more abstract level of this could be nourishment, and then physical sustenance, followed by continued life. Alternatively, starting again with our hamburger, we may move down to more detailed levels of conversation to a particular brand of hamburger, and then at a more detailed level to a particular type within that brand, such as a cheeseburger. In stepping down there are several routes we can take, and this is useful in identifying alternatives. In the hamburger example, the requirement might be for fast food when time is of the essence. An alternative might be a frozen meal, of which a healthy variety can be found. The hungry person meets his or her requirement of eating a meal that can be ready in an instant, while maintaining a healthy diet.

In determining the true requirements of the customer, we need to 'step up' to a more abstract level of conversation. To explore alternative ways of meeting that requirement, we then 'step down' to a more detailed level. For example, if a customer says that his or her requirement of the finance department is a monthly financial statement, we can 'step up' by asking 'for what purpose?' The reply might be 'to ensure I don't overspend on my budget'. This is likely to be the true requirement of the customer, and the monthly financial report merely a means of meeting this end. This is important, since the customer probably has not recognized the relative unimportance of the actual statement, and has seen it as a vital requirement. Having stepped up to identify the need to avoid overspending, we can then step down to explore alternatives. By asking, 'what else would prevent you from overspending?' we can identify alternatives that may be more appropriate and require less time to produce. In this example, real-time financial information provided on-line would meet the requirement. A process geared towards producing financial statements could then be re-engineered into a process that produces on-line information.

In practice people find it difficult to see creative alternatives that would meet the needs and requirements of the customer, usually because they mistakenly view the product that the customer receives as being the actual requirement, rather than a means of meeting the requirement. The technique of logical levelling helps people get to the true requirement by 'stepping up', and then explore alternatives by 'stepping down' through a different route.

MEASURING THE CURRENT PROCESS

While some members of the team are involved in agreeing customer requirements, other members can be busy measuring the current process. Many processes exist without valid measures of their effectiveness and efficiency. Trying to achieve breakthroughs in the performance of a process without measuring that performance is a bit like trying to alter a suit without using a tape-measure. The re-engineering team needs to be able to quantify the current process so that it can evaluate various options in the re-engineering phase: will the new process be quicker, will it use fewer resources, will it meet customer requirements better? Measurement also allows the team to benchmark the process against best-in-class alternatives, so that it can aim for truly challenging targets that exceed the performance of competitors.

Measures of the effectiveness and efficiency of the process may already exist, and the team should make use of these where possible. If they do not, and in our experience this is the most common situation, then the team can use a simple step-by-step group session to decide what it could be measuring and how it should be doing this. This session requires at least half a day, and should ideally be facilitated by an internal or external facilitator.

The first step involves the team brainstorming all the weaknesses of the current process. All ideas should then be grouped into a small number of themes, and the heading of each theme agreed. Sticky post-it notepads are ideal for this, since ideas can easily be grouped physically and positioned on a flip chart or wall. Each note should contain just one idea, which completes the sentence, 'The weaknesses of the current process are...' in a few concise words.

The second step involves the team repeating this procedure, this time for the strengths of the current process. Although simple, this activity helps clarify to the team the main features that the new process should possess, and why it is necessary to alter the current process. For example, we were recently asked to assist a re-engineering team that was meeting for the third time and where the members felt the team was losing direction. Although they had made some progress, no one knew what was really expected of them and what they should be aiming to achieve. The team consisted of people that were involved in various parts of the process, and as might be expected, they all had different views about what should be done to improve it. Simply by brainstorming the strengths and weaknesses, the team was able to see where it ought to be concentrating its attention, and started to gain an idea of what could be maintained from the current process and what needed to change for the new process. Examples of some of the ideas that were generated are:

Weaknesses

The process is paper driven
Systems very manual
Lots of paperwork passing back and forth
It is too long winded
Changes are input manually
Too much paper information to analyse quickly

Stock control not comprehensive
Raw material shortages
No finished products on accepting order

Systems not integrated
Production plans late in the day
Planning deadlines too late
Order entry too slow
Double and treble data entry

Poor control of capacity
Optimizing factory and transport difficult
Production not ready for delivery
High transport costs
Too many artificially induced peaks and troughs

Strengths

Some systems work well
Can group loads together
Historical records available
Not affected by power cuts
Easy to share written information

Proactive customer communication
Proactive ordering
Dual delivery dates

Flexible
Can be adapted locally
Easy to make minor changes
Flexible for emergency deliveries
Accommodates special requirements

Creates high level of communication
Good rapport between departments
Forces people to talk and listen
Demands good communications

Not customer responsive
We phone customers back too often
Few same day deliveries
Wrong loads sent to customers
We manipulate customer to suit us

Islands of information
Not enough usable information
Too much unusable information
Factory status information unavailable to Sales
Information never up to date
No capacity tracking
Sections can't share information on problems
Information gets lost in the system

The third step involves deciding on which aspects of the current process should be measured. For example, if a weakness of the process is that there is no comprehensive stock control system, a measure of the efficiency of the process could be the percentage of orders supplied with the correct quantity of product. Similarly, the weakness 'poor control of capacity' was measured in the above case by the number of late orders delivered to customers.

In the workshop format described here, this task is best carried out by syndicate groups from within the re-engineering team. Each syndicate should decide what facts are needed, how much data is needed, how it should be measured, and who will be responsible for collecting it.

The final step involves the syndicates reporting back their recommendations and the whole team deciding which key features of the process will be measured and used to set targets for the new process. This takes us to the next task of the re-engineering team.

DEVELOPING A VISION OF THE NEW PROCESS

In the example quoted above, a vision of the new process is what the team was principally lacking when members reported feeling unsure of the direction in which they ought to be heading. This arose partly because they had no clear understanding of the current process, and partly because they had not begun to articulate what they should be aiming for from the new process.

A useful preliminary step in formulating the vision is to benchmark the current process. After the key performance measures have been agreed, it is relatively straightforward for the team to establish challenging targets on these measures by discovering what is being achieved elsewhere. Benchmarking helps the team to do this and has several benefits. By comparing the performance of the process with that produced by competitors the team can avoid the 'not invented here' syndrome that can easily limit its effectiveness. Another benefit is that it helps motivate the team by showing what can be achieved. If used creatively it can also identify targets the team had not even considered, perhaps because it was thinking about the process too narrowly.

Benchmarking does not have to be based on the performance of competitors. Organizations that have several business units or sites where the process is in operation can gain some useful insights from internal benchmarking. A survey of 'best practices' within the company can often highlight examples of excellent performance and be a source of ideas for the format of the new process. For example, one team we worked with used this technique and found that some of the key weaknesses of a process were avoided at one site where one person had been forced to cover for two sick colleagues. Three important steps in the process that had previously been carried out by three different people were being carried out by the same person and, although this created some difficulties at the time, it overcame some of the long-standing problems experienced within the process. The re-engineering team began to consider combining tasks and roles in a way it had not considered before.

External benchmarking does not need to be limited to similar processes in competitors. Again, some of the most creative ideas for new process designs can stem from looking at industries that on the surface appear totally different. One of the best examples of this is that of a re-engineering team working in one of the international airlines. This team was re-engineering the process used to 'turn around' aircraft between flights, including cleaning the aircraft and restocking with food and fuel. In such a process time is critical, since delays have an immediate impact on customers. In considering examples of where this process is performed to the minimum of time yet to the maximum standards demanded by customers and safety requirements, this team looked beyond other airlines, and even went outside their industry. The benchmark they selected was a Formula One racing team's turnaround of cars in the pits during a race. Although different in some respects, this innovative choice captured some of the essence of their own process and allowed the re-engineering team to consider options it had not even dreamed of previously.

After the benchmarking data has been collected and reviewed, the re-engineering team should consider the strategy of the business, particularly as it relates to the process under review. There are many examples of organizations developing operational aims that conflict with the strategy of the company, or vice versa. The new process must achieve 'strategic fit' with the aims of the organization. This input into the development of the process vision can be attained in a number of ways. Written statements of strategy and strategic intent should be obtained where these are available; the annual business plan should also be consulted; it also helps enormously if a member of the Board or Executive Team can be present to give a verbal statement of the future direction of the company and how the new process is expected to contribute to this.

Finally, the requirements of customers should form the third input into the development of the process vision. These should be phrased in terms of the high-level requirements, as identified through the technique of logical levelling, rather than specific requirements that are likely to be the means by which these high-level requirements are met.

The vision statement should be capable of transforming the overall strategy into actions that will contribute to the achievement of that strategy. To do this the statement should contain specific objectives that are measurable and which are based on the performance measures that will have been developed earlier by the team. It should also contain statements of the specific attributes of the new process, which will show how the process will operate, who it will involve, and where it will be performed.

At this stage the team needs to gather ideas on what these objectives and attributes might be, without being too concerned about their validity. Hence an initial brainstorming session is a helpful way of doing this. Armed with the three inputs of benchmarking data, customer requirements and business strategy, the re-engineering team should hold a brainstorming session to generate a large number of ideas about what the new process should achieve and the form it should take. The topic might be something like: 'All the things we want the new process to be'. This will produce a list of ideas that should then be subjected to more rigorous analysis. The first step in doing this is to group the ideas into general themes. In practice these themes are likely to reflect broad areas like 'customers', 'technology', 'organizational' and 'cost'. These broad areas can be allocated to small groups from within the team, whose brief will be to take the ideas and develop specific objectives and attributes of the new process.

The final step in the visioning process is to formulate a written vision statement. This should take into account the work performed by the syndicate groups in stating objectives and attributes, and is usually best carried out by one or two people. In some respects a process vision statement resembles an organizational vision statement, and anyone who has been involved in writing the latter will know that this can be a difficult and challenging task. In producing a draft version of the process vision, several guidelines can be used to ensure that the vision effectively captures the work completed so far by the re-engineering team and that it fulfils the requirements of the team at this stage.

STATE THE VISION IN THE POSITIVE

A common trap that teams can fall into is stating what the process will not do rather than what it will do. Phrases like 'with zero defects' or 'with no customer complaints' are good examples of this trap, and should be avoided. It is far better for the vision to motivate people to achieve something positive than to avoid something negative, and this should be reflected in the wording that is chosen. Even if this trap is avoided, words like 'reduce', 'shorten', 'minimize', and so on, should be replaced by phrases that state what will be achieved rather than what will be lost or reduced.

STATE THE EVIDENCE

The vision should contain statements, the results of which can be measured and which will allow a clear and unambiguous judgement of whether the vision has been achieved or not. Ideally, these statements should contain more than just numbers, since this will have the effect of making the vision more real and attractive for those performing the process. A study of Neuro Linguistic Programming shows that objectives that appeal to the five human senses are much more likely to motivate people than bland facts and figures. Thus there could be reference to the visual aspects of the process, what customers might say about it, and the feelings it will generate. All of these should clearly indicate the evidence that is required for the vision to be judged to have been achieved.

SPECIFY THE CONTEXT

The vision statement should be specific and cover the context in which it will apply. It should therefore include the *who*, *what*, *where* and *how* of the new process. All too often vision statements contain woolly, 'apple pie' and 'motherhood' sentiments that have little obvious relevance to the work of those who will be trying to achieve the vision. The more specific the statement, the more likely it is to be seen as a practical and realistic goal to strive for.

STATE HOW THE VISION WILL BE INITIATED AND MAINTAINED BY THOSE WHO WILL ACHIEVE IT

Statements divorced from the actions and intent of the people on whom they depend can easily be seen as out of their control and influence. Under these conditions, people feel powerless to shape the outcome of the process, and feel that the vision is something that might be achieved if luck is on their side or if others look favourably upon them. To avoid this the vision statement should contain a clear indication of how the actions of those operating the process will contribute to the achievement of the vision.

ENSURE THE STATEMENT IS ECOLOGICALLY SOUND

It is not uncommon for missions and objectives to implicitly create the opposite of what they are intended to achieve. This occurs when they conflict with other goals and values. A mission to maximize profit, for example, may mean job losses, unpleasant working conditions, strict regimes and environmental damage. In constructing a statement of the process vision, the team should ensure that it contains objectives that are consistent with other goals within the organization, and that the achievement of the vision will have positive and not negative effects on other parts of the business.

If the re-engineering team has analysed fully the current process and created a vision of what the new process will be like, they will avoid the common experience of lacking understanding and direction that so often plagues teams in the early stages of process re-engineering. They will be ready to move on to the next stage, which is that of mapping the current process as a prelude to developing the new, re-engineered process.

8 Mapping the Process

One of the key tools used in re-engineering a process is a map of that process. A map allows the team to see all parts of the process and how those parts fit together, and the weaknesses and unnecessary complexities of the process will often be revealed, along with any strengths that may need to be preserved in the new process. The process map also enables the team to design different alternatives to the current process and to compare these before deciding which one to adopt. Sophisticated software packages allow key parameters to be fed into these process designs, and are capable of highlighting possible bottlenecks that may occur or simply showing the volume of work that can be achieved within these parameters.

In this chapter we will outline a technique for mapping complex processes. The technique overcomes some of the weaknesses associated with flow-charting, and enables a team to plan which parts of a process to re-engineer and which parts to improve using less radical changes. In this way the team can achieve the best of both worlds, combining traditional process change with more radical process re-engineering.

Traditionally, flow charts have been used to represent on paper the main steps involved in a process. Unfortunately, this technique was developed before the advent of process re-engineering and so is not equipped to deal with the complexity and sheer size of processes that span many departments. The difficulty is akin to using A to Z street guides to produce a map of the world. What is needed is a technique that can capture complexity in a process and represent it in a simple and uncluttered map.

STRUCTURED PROCESS ANALYSIS

The technique called Structured Process Analysis (SPA) was developed by our consultant team and uses principles from the world of data modelling. It is based on the principle of a process hierarchy. As we have seen, a process can be broken down into its constituent sub-processes.

Where the process in question is one that spans several departments, then these sub-processes are likely to be fairly complex themselves, and may include the work carried out by more than one department. We can further divide each sub-process into main activities and these in turn can be broken down into specific tasks. For example, the process of recruiting a new employee will contain the sub-process of advertising the vacancy, which in turn will include the activity of producing a job and person specification. This in turn will include specific tasks such as typing the specifications.

Structured Process Analysis reflects this hierarchy, and works like a series of geographical maps that differ in their level of detail and scope. To return to the analogy of street guides, we would start our map of the world with an atlas that simply showed the continents and the countries that made up these continents. If we wanted to know more about the detail of any of the countries, we could consult a map of that country, which would show the main towns, cities, and arterial links. For each city we could then consult a detailed street guide. For a given road in this guide we could refer to local town plans, which would show the position of houses along that road. In principle, an architect's drawing of a house could then be obtained, showing the location of rooms within that building. Thus we would have a hierarchy of maps that would start at the level of continents and progress down to the plan of a bathroom!

In Structured Process Analysis, a complex process is represented by data flow diagrams showing different levels of detail in much the same way as the above example. A data flow diagram is a simple way of showing the flow of inputs and outputs. At the level of specific tasks, such as producing a job specification, flow charts can be used to illustrate the steps involved, decisions made, and the input of information or the movement of goods. A few examples will show the strength of this technique and its many uses, and also the potential pitfalls that a team needs to avoid.

PROCESS ENVIRONMENT DIAGRAMS

Initially, the process is represented only by a circle, in what is called a process environment diagram. This diagram should also show the main customers and suppliers of the process, represented by oblong boxes, and the flow of inputs and outputs to and from the process, represented by arrowed lines. The example shown in Figure 8.1 represents the 'order fulfilment' process of a company producing animal feed bought by farmers for their cows and pigs.

At this level simplicity is the key, and the team needs to avoid adding too much detail. A common mistake that teams make is that of repre-

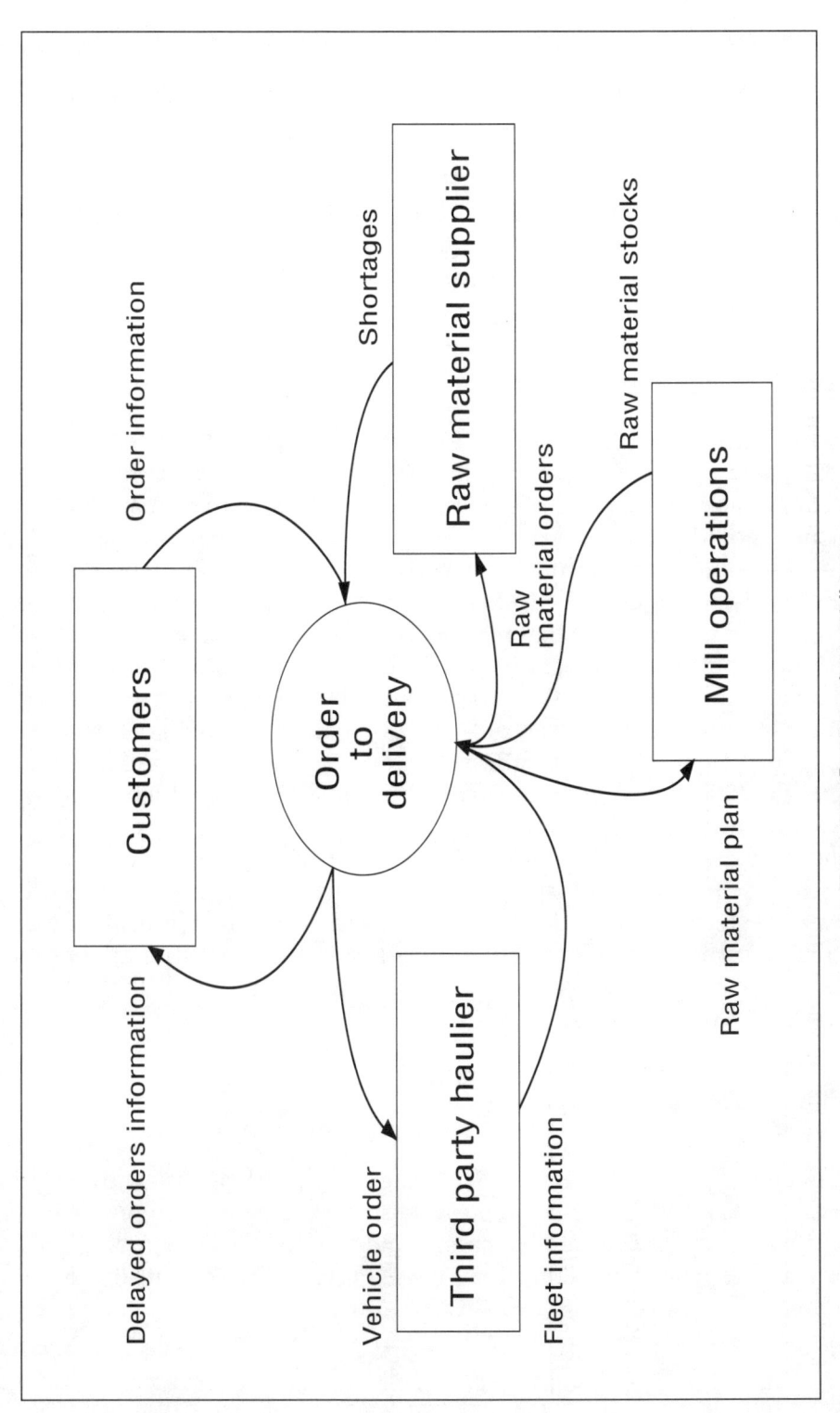

Figure 8.1 Process environment diagram

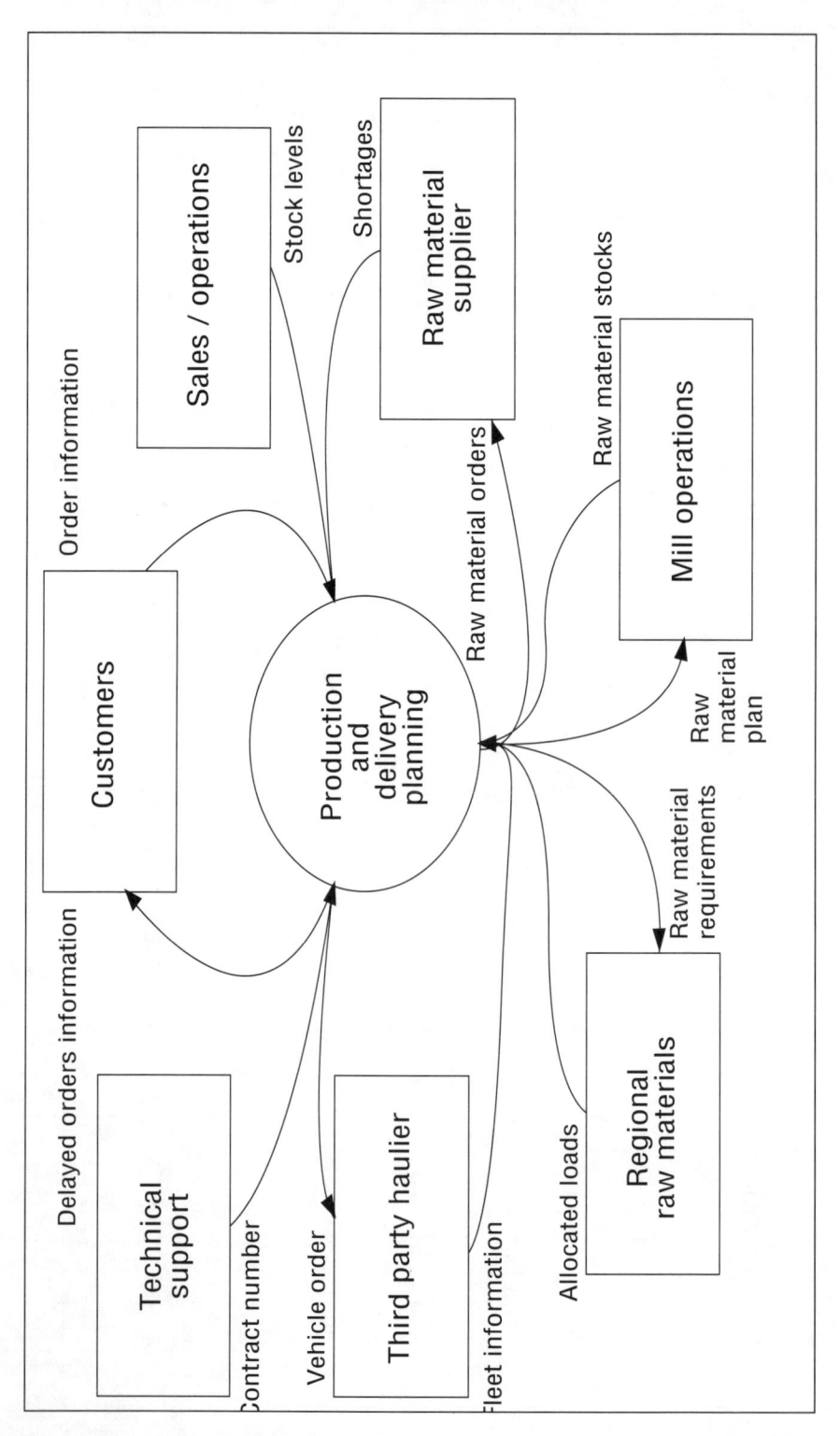

A PRACTICAL GUIDE TO BUSINESS PROCESS RE-ENGINEERING

Figure 8.2 Original process environment diagram

senting sub-processes as separate processes. As we stated in Chapter 6, teams often have difficulty in defining a process in truly cross-functional terms and tend to see processes too narrowly, rather than as parts of a larger process. Hence they are more likely to draw their process environment diagram at a lower level of detail than is required. In terms of our analogy with geographical maps, they see and draw countries, rather than continents. This occurred with the team re-engineering the process shown in Figure 8.1. They began by defining the process as that of 'production and delivery planning', and produced a process environment diagram that looked like that in Figure 8.2. This limited the team in the options it had to re-engineer this process, since many departments and processes were considered outside its scope. In general, broadening the process scope to include sub-processes that are performed in different departments not only increases the scale of organizational change involved in the re-engineering project, it also dramatically increases the scale of the benefits that are likely to be gained.

DATA FLOW DIAGRAMS

Having agreed on the process environment diagram, the team should then produce a process map that presents an exploded view of the process represented so far as only a circle. This is the first-level data flow diagram, and shows the main sub-processes that constitute the process. Each sub-process is represented by a circle, with the flow of inputs and outputs being shown by annotated arrow lines. There is no need to include the customers and suppliers shown in the process environment diagram, merely the inputs and outputs to and from them. Hence overcomplexity in the process map is avoided by only showing new information. For the process shown in Figure 8.1, the first-level data flow diagram should look like that shown in Figure 8.3. The main steps involved in the process would therefore be as follows:

- Step 1: The Customer Services Department receives an order from a customer, records this, and sends it to the Sales and Operations Department and a copy to the Technical Support Department.
- Step 2: Using information on customer orders, the Technical Support Department produces technical information relating to the type of product mix required and sends this to the Sales and Operations Department
- Step 3: Using information on customer orders and technical information, a sales order is produced by the Sales and Operations Department, along with information on current stock levels. This information is sent to the Production Planner.

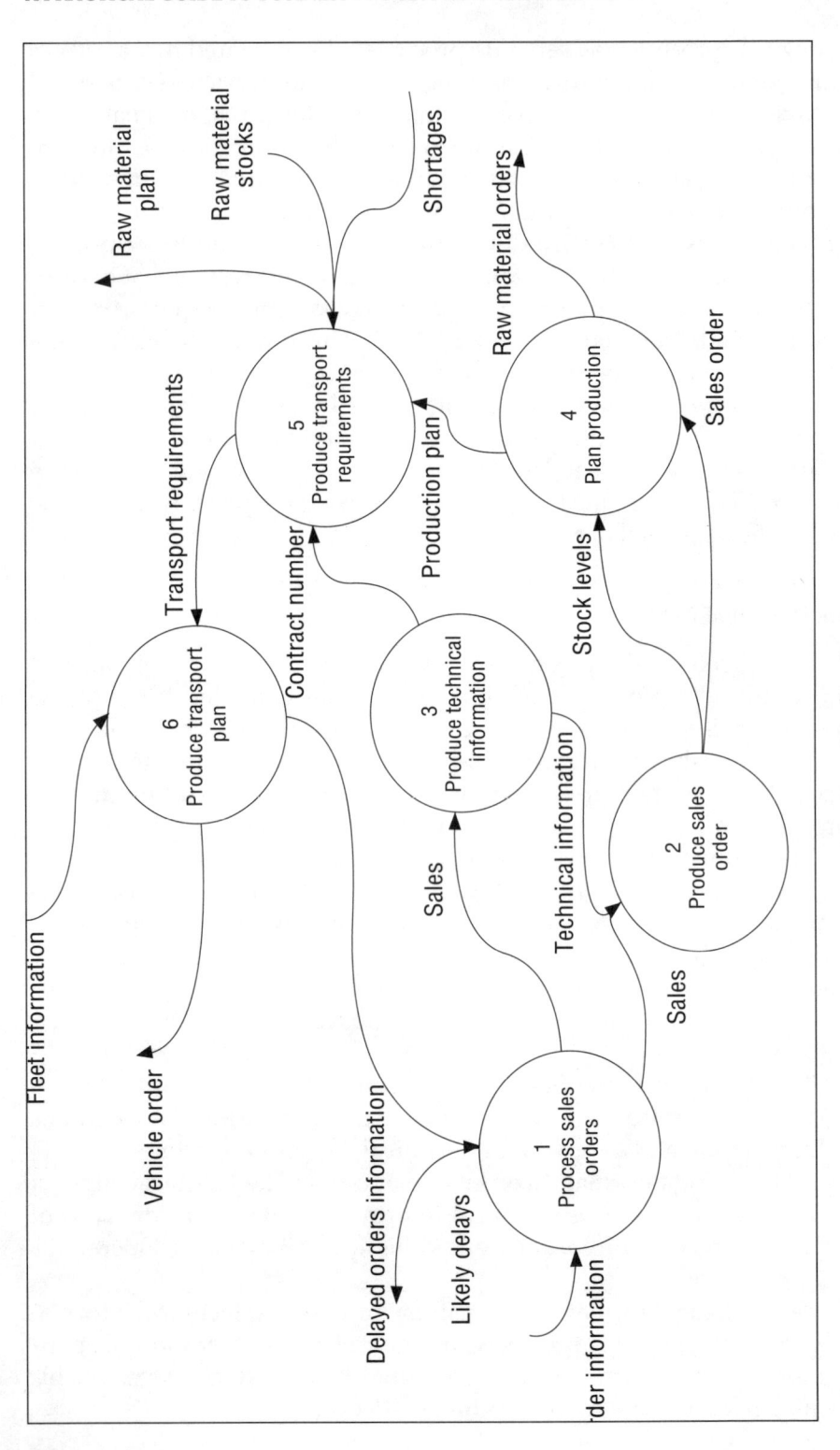

Figure 8.3 Data flow diagram

MAPPING THE PROCESS

- Step 4: A production plan is produced for the Raw Material Planning Department. This is done using sales and stock information.
- Step 5: The Raw Material Planning Department use the production plan, a contract number, and details of the availability of transport and raw material stocks, to produce transport requirements and a raw material plan.
- Step 6: Using the transport requirements and fleet information from a third party haulier, the Transport Planner produces an order for a vehicle. Information on delays are produced for the Customer Services Department.

Following these steps, Mill Operations produce the required amount of stock, ready for collection from the haulier. The haulier collects the product and delivers it to the customer.

This data flow diagram shows the main sub-processes involved in this process, and how these are linked to produce the primary output of the process, which in this case is animal food transported direct to a farmer. It provides a helicopter view of the process, although it does not give any details of the main steps involved in each sub-process. More often than not, in our experience, this is the first time the complete process has been mapped for all involved in it to see. Individual members of the team are likely to have been involved in producing the map, giving

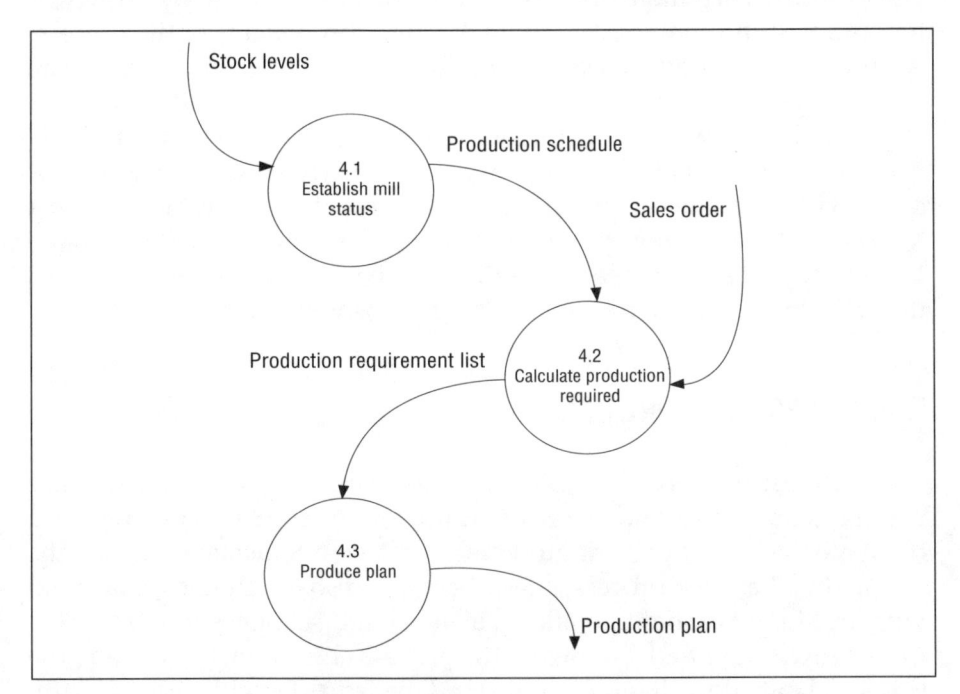

Figure 8.4   Second-level data flow diagram

details of their role in the process, but it is unlikely that they will have had a very clear picture of each other's role.

Substantial re-engineering of the process is likely to occur at this level, and may involve removing sub-processes, or combining several sub-processes into one. However, in order to make these decisions, the team needs to have more information on what actually goes on within each sub-process. Hence there is a need for more detail than is contained on this first-level data flow diagram, and this is achieved by producing second-level diagrams.

The second-level data flow diagrams are produced by taking each circle, and exploding it into its main elements. This produces a series of diagrams, equal in number to the number of circles shown in the first-level diagram. Each diagram represents the main elements of the sub-process it is detailing, shown once again as a data flow diagram.

DATA FLOW LEVELLING

In this way a three-dimensional map, showing the process, its sub-processes, and so on, is constructed. A second-level data flow diagram, based on Step 4 of Figure 8.3, is shown in Figure 8.4. This identifies the main steps involved in Step 4, each represented by a circle with inputs and outputs. The whole process can thus be broken down by this levelling process into successively more detailed components of the process. A flow chart should be used rather than a data flow diagram where the main steps to be mapped are individual actions and decisions. Structured Process Analysis therefore begins at the highest level with a process environment diagram, proceeds down successive levels of detail with data flow diagrams, and concludes at the lowest level with a flow chart. We will shortly describe some of the principles of flow-charting, but first there is a need to outline some of the potential difficulties involved in SPA and some guidelines to help avoid these.

GUIDELINES FOR USING SPA

There is clearly a need for clarity and rigour in using SPA if the re-engineering team is to avoid errors or confusion over the process map and there are several important guidelines that help to achieve this c... :ity. The first is that each process, sub-process, and so on, should be labelled with a unique number that allows its level and sequence in the process to be clearly identified. Following the process environment diagram, the first-level data flow diagram should be labelled as Level 1, and each sub-process numbered in sequence (1, 2, 3, etc.). At the next level of detail,

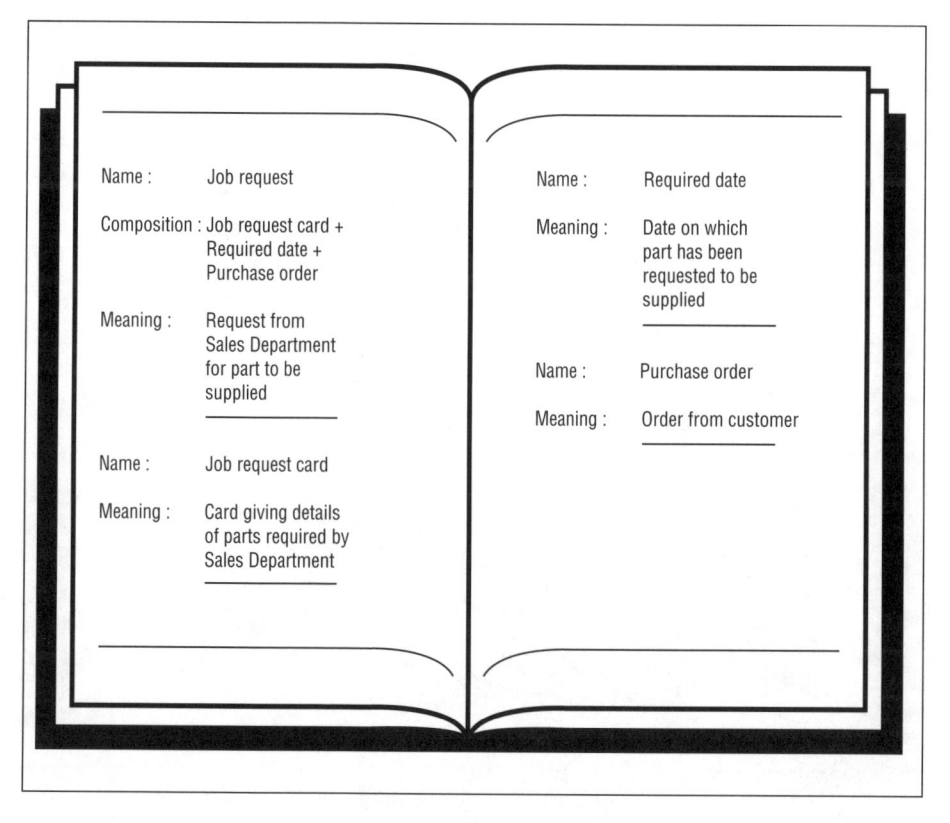

Figure 8.5 Process dictionary

Name :	Job request
Composition :	Job request card + Required date + Purchase order
Meaning :	Request from Sales Department for part to be supplied
Name :	Job request card
Meaning :	Card giving details of parts required by Sales Department
Name :	Required date
Meaning :	Date on which part has been requested to be supplied
Name :	Purchase order
Meaning :	Order from customer

each sub-process should have its main steps numbered as subscripts. Thus if sub-process 1 is broken down into three steps, these should be numbered 1.1, 1.2, 1.3. The two steps that might constitute sub-process 2 would be numbered 2.1 and 2.2, and so on. At the level of detail below this, the two parts of step 1.1 would be numbered 1.1.1 and 1.1.2. In this way we can easily identify the level of detail, the sequence, and the main sub-process that any part of the whole process belongs to. This notation is similar to that of numbering the sections, and sub-subsections of a document using a 'legal' format.

A second guideline is to create a process dictionary, where each input and output is defined in precise terms. As with our hierarchy of process levels, the composition of an input or output can also be defined in terms of elements which themselves may form the inputs and outputs of sub-processes. Thus a 'job request' may be defined as a request from the sales department for the production of a specific part. It may consist of a job request card, a copy of a purchase order, and a required date. Each of these three elements should also be defined within the dictionary, so that there is little if any room for misinterpretation (*see* Figure 8.5). Although

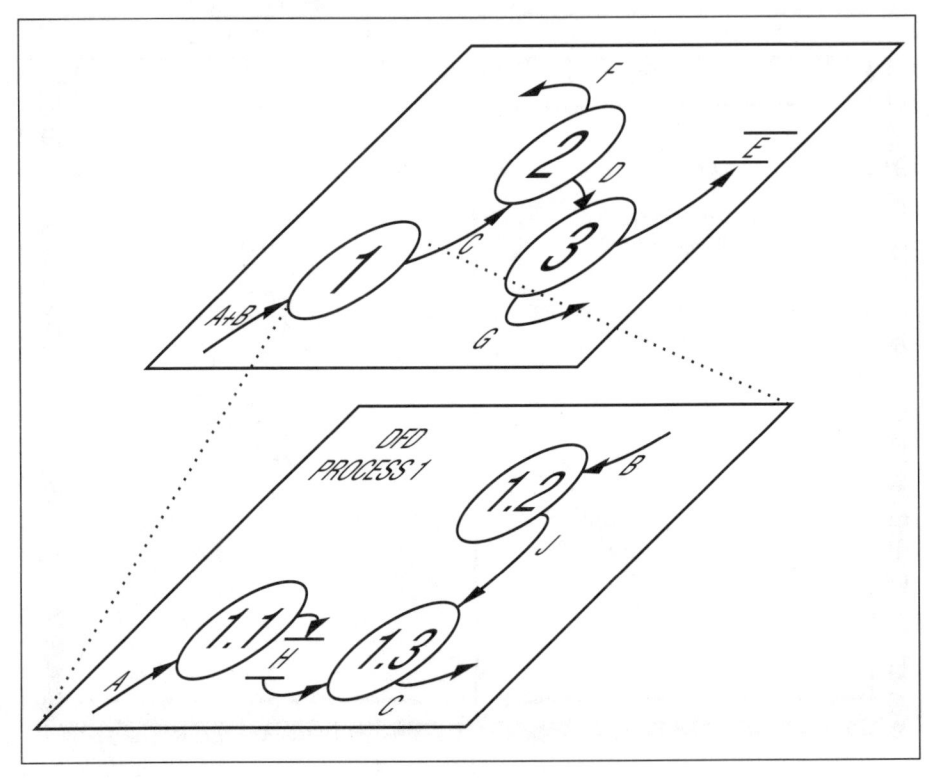

Figure 8.6 Input/output consistency

this may seem a somewhat bureaucratic task, there are software packages that allow the dictionary to be constructed in quite an easy manner, and which ensure that no terms are entered as part of any definition unless they are defined in the dictionary.

The process dictionary is often an important tool to prevent confusion and errors which can occur if different but similar outputs are described using the same terms. It is especially important where a complex process is being analysed and there is some similarity between inputs and outputs. To give a simple but nevertheless useful example, a team set up by a building society to re-engineer its internal distribution process produced a process map which seemed to indicate internal post travelling to and from various sites for no apparent reason. Upon closer inspection it transpired the team had used the label 'post' to refer to both sorted and unsorted mail. In fact unsorted post was an input into a process of sorting the mail, and sorted post was the output of this process, though the map gave no indication of this step.

Finally, a third guideline in using SPA is the need to maintain input/output consistency between different levels of detail. In essence, this means that the number of inputs and outputs to a process should be the same between levels. For example, in Figure 8.6 there are two inputs into sub-process 1, and one output. When this sub-process is exploded into a lower-level data flow diagram, there must also be just these two inputs and one output, shown as loose-ended arrowed lines. Within the main steps at this level there may be additional inputs and outputs, but these will not be loose-ended since they will link the steps at this level. In Figure 8.6, if sub-process 1.1 was broken down to a further level of detail, we would expect there to be one input and one output, though once again the steps within this sub-process could be linked by additional inputs and outputs.

Maintaining input/output consistency ensures the internal accuracy of the data flow diagrams. In breaking a process down to a lower level of detail, it is quite easy to overlook inputs and outputs that have been identified at the higher level. Conversely, people sometimes identify inputs and outputs at this detailed level which were overlooked when drawing the higher-level diagram. In this case the team should add these to the higher-level diagram.

FLOW CHARTS

We have mentioned flow charts at several points in this chapter, and will now say a little more about what these are and how they can be used in conjunction with data flow diagrams. We do not see SPA replacing flow charts but rather that it includes these as the final level of detail required when mapping a complex process. As we shall see towards the end of this chapter, a combination of both data flow diagrams and flow charts can realize significant benefits.

Flow charts have been with us for many years, and this testifies to the power of the technique. However, process re-engineering involves change on a larger scale than that which traditionally has been envisaged, and for which flow charts were originally devised. To return to our geographical analogy, street maps may be helpful for a town planning department deciding how to improve the flow of traffic around a town centre, but are of little use in redrawing national and pan-national boundaries on the scale that has been witnessed in Europe in recent years.

Flow charts, then, are visual representations of the steps involved in a process, and are mostly used at the level of detail that involves specific tasks, actions, and decisions. Symbols are used to represent the process. Although there are a number of different symbols that can be used, the most common are those shown in Figure 8.7, and these will be sufficient for most teams to capture the detail of a low-level process. Some readers may be familiar with the perspex stencil that enables these symbols to be

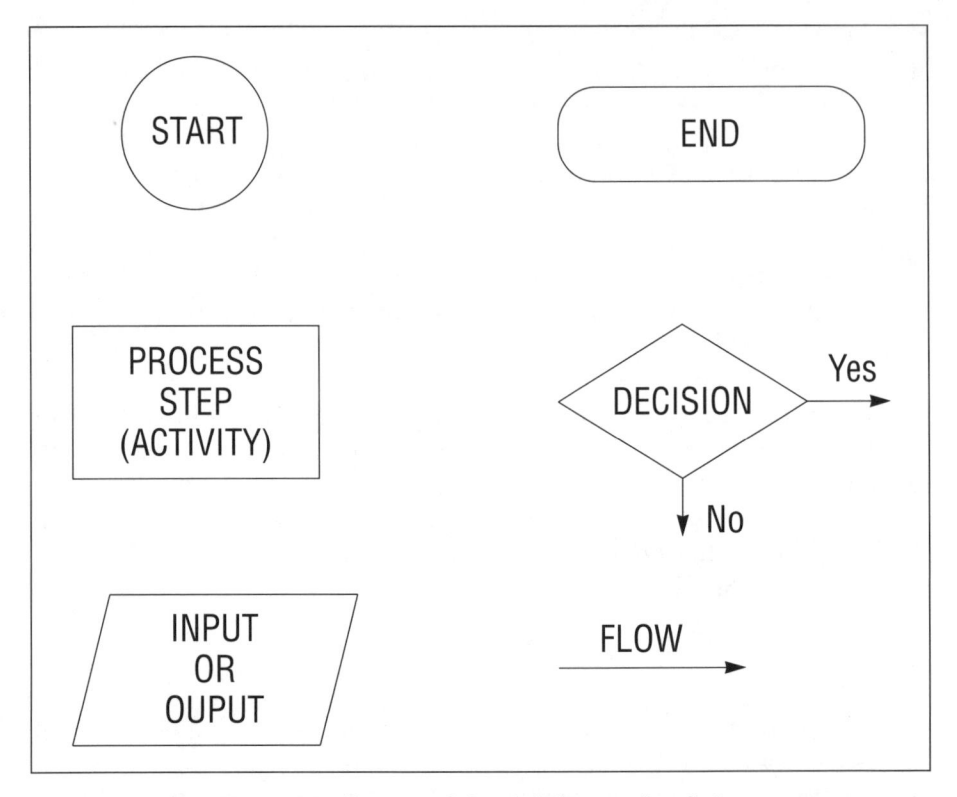

```
┌─────────────────────────────────────────────────┐
│                                                 │
│      ( START )              ( END )             │
│                                                 │
│                                                 │
│   ┌──────────┐                                  │
│   │ PROCESS  │                 ◇  Yes           │
│   │  STEP    │            ◇ DECISION ◇──→       │
│   │(ACTIVITY)│                 ◇                │
│   └──────────┘                 │ No             │
│                                ▼                │
│                                                 │
│     ╱ INPUT  ╱                                  │
│    ╱   OR   ╱            FLOW ───→              │
│   ╱ OUPUT  ╱                                    │
│                                                 │
└─────────────────────────────────────────────────┘
```

Figure 8.7 Recommended symbols for use on flow charts

drawn neatly and accurately and which can easily be carried around in one's briefcase, although once again there are now software programs that make the task of drawing a flow chart much easier.

As with SPA, drawing a flow chart may appear a little difficult at first, but people soon develop a knack for doing this quickly and accurately. Although the final version should be drawn using a computer program, the initial drafts are usually best produced on large pieces of flip chart paper where everyone in the group can contribute. It is sensible to have someone who has used the technique before to facilitate this session and to be the scribe. Once again there are guidelines that help ensure the team uses the technique properly and gets the most out of it.

One simple guideline is that each action step in the process, represented by a rectangle, should begin with a verb to reflect that it is an action. However, one common problem is that people often use general verbs to describe what they do within a process, and this can obscure the actual steps and actions involved. For instance, someone who says that the next step in the process is 'gather relevant data' may unwittingly conceal the fact that this actually involves a whole series of actions and people. Remember that 'gather relevant data' is likely to be a sub-process in itself, and should have been represented in a previously drawn data flow diagram as a circle with various inputs showing the data and their sources, and an output which may be a report or a recommendation. At the level of flow-charting, however, more detail is required to show the steps, people and decisions that are involved in this task. One way of getting down to this level of detail is to ask, "how do you do that?" So in this example the facilitator should ask, 'how do you gather relevant data?' This will usually reveal the detail that is involved in the task, and each step should then be recorded using the correct flow-charting symbols.

Another common problem is that when people describe the steps of a process, they often represent the process in an idealized way. They describe what *should* happen if everything goes according to plan, not what *does* happen when events and people seem to conspire to wreck these plans. A facilitator or other team members not familiar with this part of the process may not realize that important steps will have been omitted. Obviously this will make it difficult to improve the process once it has been represented in this idealized way, since on paper at least, the process may appear to be operating without unexpected hitches and delays.

Once again there is a simple way to avoid this problem. The facilitator should ask, 'does that always happen next' or 'are there ever any things that go wrong and which make that next step more complicated?' Usually this is greeted with cries of 'all the time!' and once again the team can describe in detail what normally happens and capture this in the flow chart.

Finally, a 'decision step', represented by a diamond with 'yes' or 'no' outputs, should not be confined only to those stages in the process where a conscious and deliberate decision is made, such as 'does this meet the quality standard?' Very often decision steps are useful ways of capturing what can often go wrong in a process and the additional activities that are required to put them right. For example, when we were working with a team of hospital porters who were trying to improve the process of getting patients to and from the operating theatres, the team stated that after arriving at the ward their first action was to help get the patient on the trolley. When our consultant asked if this was always the first thing they did upon arriving, they pointed out that it depended on whether the patient was on the ward or not. Hence a decision step labelled 'Is patient on ward?' was added. The 'no' output led to a number of options, depending on whether the porter had been sent to the wrong ward, whether the patient had wandered off to the toilet, and so on. Each option was in turn represented by a decision step.

It transpired that there were regular delays resulting from patients not

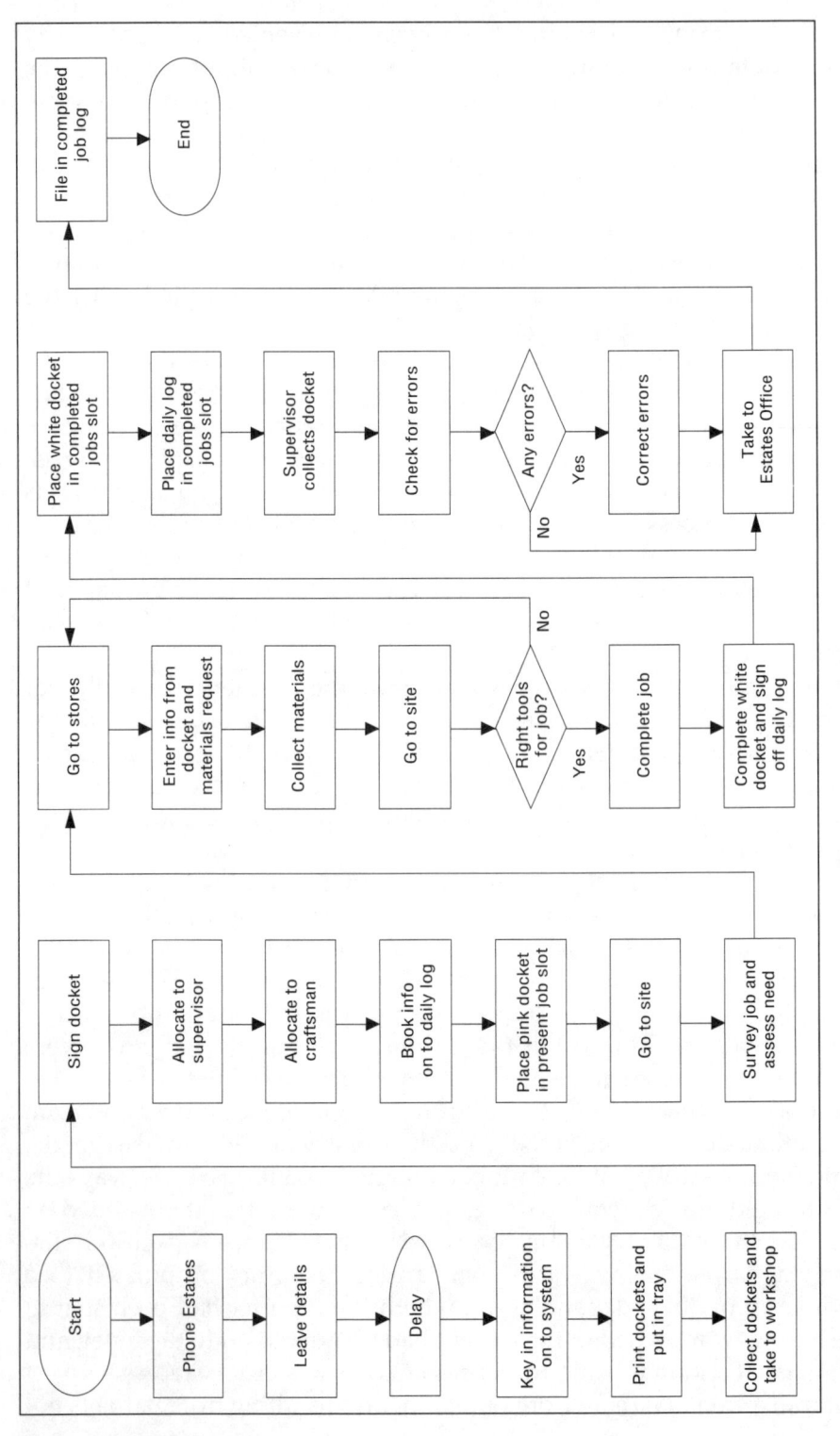

A PRACTICAL GUIDE TO BUSINESS PROCESS RE-ENGINEERING

Figure 8.8 Flow chart for job repair process

MAPPING THE PROCESS

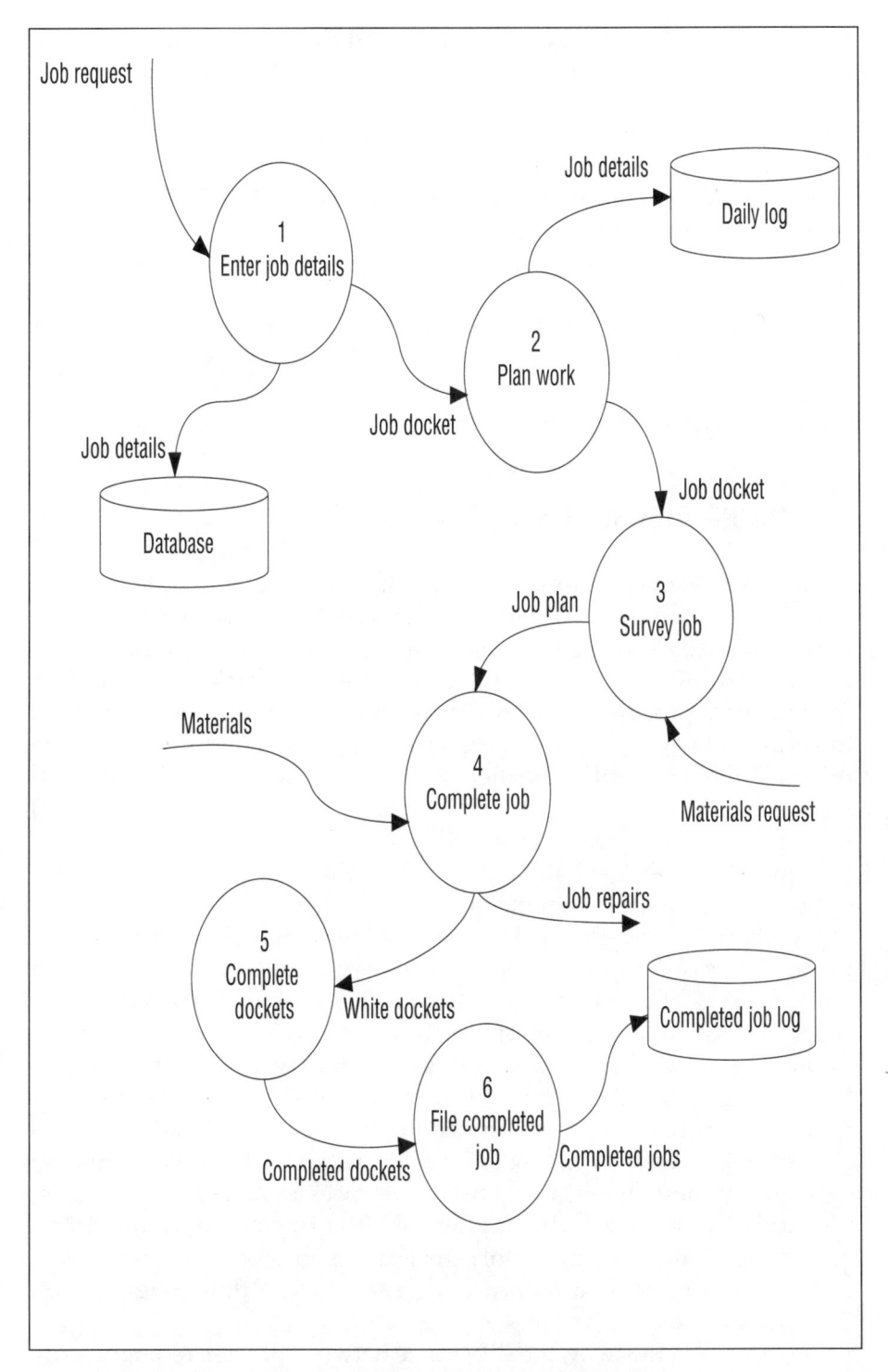

Figure 8.9 Data flow diagram for job repair process

being ready and waiting on the ward, and that to find the patient the porters would have to perform a number of additional tasks, such as telephoning operating theatres to check the details, looking around the ward and those wards in the immediate vicinity, and so on. Sometimes these delays resulted in operations being cancelled, with the significant costs and patient complaints that often followed. This fault within the process could easily have been omitted if the decision step was used only to show the formal decisions that are made during a process. In fact the number of *ad hoc* decisions that are routinely made in any process was highlighted in this case by the head porter, who surveyed the completed flow chart represented on pages of flip chart paper posted on the wall and quipped, 'I never realized I made so many decisions in my job, I reckon I'm due a pay rise!'

MAXIMIZING THE USE OF SPA

Although SPA may seem like a difficult technique at first, teams very quickly learn how to draw data flow diagrams and flow charts, and how to use these to change and improve a process. We will see in the next chapter how SPA can be used in conjunction with various principles to re-engineer a process, but at this stage an SPA map may be viewed as a three-dimensional picture of a process. Like flow-charting on its own, this is often a useful aid when it comes to redesigning a process. However, it is when used in conjunction with flow charts that the full strength of the technique can be realized.

Using the high-level data flow diagrams, the team can consider options which require significant changes in how a process is carried out, without being concerned with the details of its sub-processes. Once the team has developed optional processes it can look in detail at what remains of the old process, using low-level data flow diagrams and flow charts to streamline and improve these. In this way the team avoids improving detailed parts of a process which may ultimately disappear following the re-engineering that occurs at a higher level. Only those parts of the process that remain need to be streamlined and improved. Hence for a process consisting of five sub-processes, a team may re-engineer this by combining the first two sub-processes into one, outsourcing the third to a supplier, and changing the fifth to include substantial steps performed by the customer. Only the fourth sub-process would remain, and so the team should then use lower-level data flow diagrams and flow charts of this sub-process to improve it.

Thought of in this way, the difference between process re-engineering and process improvement can be operationally defined in terms of the level in the SPA hierarchy at which changes are made. At the lowest level, using flow charts, any changes will be fine detail improvements and streamlining. As we move up the hierarchy, changes become more and more significant, with genuine re-engineering occurring when we change the nature of the first-level data flow diagram.

Another benefit of moving up and down this process hierarchy to make changes to a process concerns the difficulties that teams often experience in terms of thinking big enough to bring about quantum or 'step' improvements rather than smooth continuous improvements. This problem is compounded by the level of detail at which the team often views the process, since each person in the re-engineering team will probably be very familiar with their part of the process. In such situations it helps enormously to move up a level, and view the process at a more abstract level.

The benefits of taking a more abstract view are highlighted in the following example, which is based on a flow chart that a maintenance team at a university produced for the process of responding to requests for repairs to equipment used in the laboratories (*see* Figure 8.8). Although this team was not attempting to re-engineer the process they nevertheless experienced some difficulty in achieving anything other than piecemeal changes to what was patently an overly bureaucratic process and one which constantly prompted jokes within other departments about how many maintenance engineers were required to change a light bulb!

The problem was that the flow chart showed too much detail, and the breakthrough came when the team produced a higher-level data flow diagram that showed more clearly the various parties involved in the process without all of the detail of what tasks they performed (*see* Figure 8.9). The team was able to see a number of different options, based on taking people out of this process and combining tasks. As well as improving dramatically the time taken to respond to requests for repairs, their solution had the added benefit of reducing the number of jokes about how many of them were required to do this!

By moving up the process hierarchy a team is therefore able to make more substantial, radical and far-reaching changes to a process where this is required. SPA, in representing a process as a series of maps arranged in a hierarchy, enables a team to do this, while at the same time allowing it to move down the hierarchy to improve and streamline those parts of the process that remain after such drastic 'surgery'.

9 Tools

At this stage the re-engineering team will probably know more about the process than any other group within the organization. Process maps will have been drawn of all the main sub-processes and so on; performance statistics enabling it to be benchmarked against internal and external competition will exist, along with a vision of how the new process should perform and the customer requirements it will fulfil. Armed with this information, the team is now ready to start the task of designing a new process. A number of practical tools can be used which will enable the team to achieve its task. In this chapter we will describe these tools and the steps the team needs to follow in the re-engineering phase.

THE ROLE OF CREATIVITY IN PROCESS RE-ENGINEERING

Although the concept of re-designing a new process unfettered by any of the assumptions that guide its current form is an attractive one, it is rarely applied to its full extent. One of the reasons for this is that individuals and teams can find it extraordinarily difficult to think in such a creative way. By definition, creative thinking is seeing things in a new way, developing ideas that have not previously existed. In general, most organizations do little to promote this, and the average person has had little coaching or development in this key skill.

Psychologists have defined creativity in terms of four different components, and it is helpful to understand what these are and how they can be observed in work situations if we are to apply them to process re-engineering.

The first component is *similarity*, which usually involves seeing links between things that others have not perceived. The example of the benchmarking team that saw a link between a Formula One pit stop and an aircraft turn-around illustrates this.

The second component is *alternative functions*, which is the ability to see different uses of the same thing. A good example of this type of thinking was provided by a team of hospital consultants who were looking at ways of reducing the number of people failing to attend medical appointments. Their solution was to ask patients to phone in and make their own appointment, rather than leave this task to a medical secretary. Although people normally make their own appointments for dental treatment or even haircuts, no one had seen it as an alternative way for hospital appointments to be made. Appointments made by the patients themselves were obviously timed to fit around their own schedules and were thus less likely to be missed.

The third component is *number of instances*, and involves perceiving many different instances of a common theme. In work-based problem-solving, this type of creativity can be seen when many different causes, some not at all obvious, are identified as contributing to a problem. It is often through tackling the cause no one has previously recognized that the problem is finally solved.

An example of this type of thinking comes from a company we worked with in the food distribution business. A problem-solving team of warehouse staff was attempting to reduce the number of incorrect orders that were shipped to supermarkets. Most errors were due to the wrong sized items being sent, costing the company many hundreds of thousands of pounds a year. The problem had no obvious cause other than human error: fork lift truck operators would lift a pallet of large tins of beans, say, instead of small tins. The problem was solved when it was recognized that the root cause was an unwritten assumption that the warehouse should be stocked in just the same way as the supermarkets it supplied, with goods arranged in product families. This meant that errors could easily occur, since all sizes were stored in close proximity to each other. The team's solution was to keep different sizes in different parts of the warehouse. This solution came about only because the team was able to generate a previously unrecognized cause of the problem, and not consider only the obvious one of human error.

The fourth component is *naming*, and this involves generating many different interpretations of the same thing. In work situations naming requires the ability to see something from different viewpoints and to generate opportunities from this. An example of this comes from a team in the publishing industry that found that 'printing defects' was the most common cause of production-related problems. Yet reducing the number of these defects did not result in the hoped-for financial benefits that management had expected from this problem-solving team. This was because the team was looking at production problems from one viewpoint only: frequency. Instead of asking 'what problems happen most often?' the team later asked the question, 'what problems cost the most money to put right?' This led to print overruns being identified as the most costly problem, even though it had not been the most common problem.

In re-engineering a process, a team needs to draw upon all of these ways of being creative; to draw ideas from other, apparently unrelated, processes to develop new ways of doing things; to develop new ways of using existing resources, be they human or technical; and to consider new outputs that would meet the customers' requirements in better ways than the outputs created by the current process. There are some techniques that can help a team to do all of these things, yet these techniques can really be effective only if they are accompanied by the right 'mind set'. An important role for the facilitator of the re-engineering team is therefore to help create this state of psychological readiness for creative thinking.

One of the ways in which this can be done is to use various exercises that highlight and emphasize the role of creativity in the team's task. One such useful exercise is the puzzle of five pigeons on a roof, one of which is shot dead by a hunter. How many are left? The most common immediate answer is four. After a few seconds people realize that the four live pigeons are likely to have flown away following the noise of the gunshot, and so offer an alternative: the dead pigeon is the only one left. Most people are happy to stop at this answer. However, if pressed for additional answers, various solutions from none to five can be constructed based on possibilities such as pigeons staying behind to grieve the loss of their dead friend, or flying it away to the great pigeon graveyard in the sky. Most people stop here, believing they have given every possible answer. If they are asked for new answers they look bewildered. How can there possibly be any other numbers they have not mentioned? After a few seconds someone usually recognizes that the number can be greater than five, and offers an answer based on other pigeons arriving on the scene. People soon recognize there can be any number of answers to the problem, limited only by the creativity of their minds.

The exercise, based on the 'number of instances' component of creativity, can be used to make a useful point: that people usually develop only a limited number of obvious solutions to a problem and that without any additional encouragement they often stop at this point, believing there can be no other solutions. The importance of pressing for new alternatives, even if it seems there can't possibly be any, is the central message of the exercise. In a similar manner, the re-engineering team should not only consider the obvious alternatives but explore previously unthought of options, recognizing that these options exist but will not be recognized without additional thought.

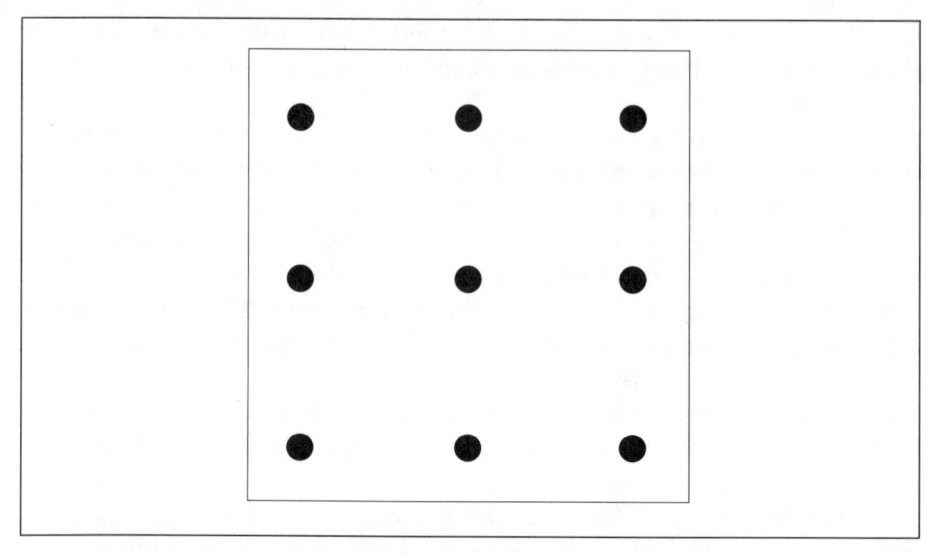

Figure 9.1 Nine-dot problem

Another exercise that could be used is the well-known nine-dot problem (*see* Figure 9.1). The aim here is to join all nine dots by drawing only four straight lines. The solution shown in Figure 9.2 demonstrates the

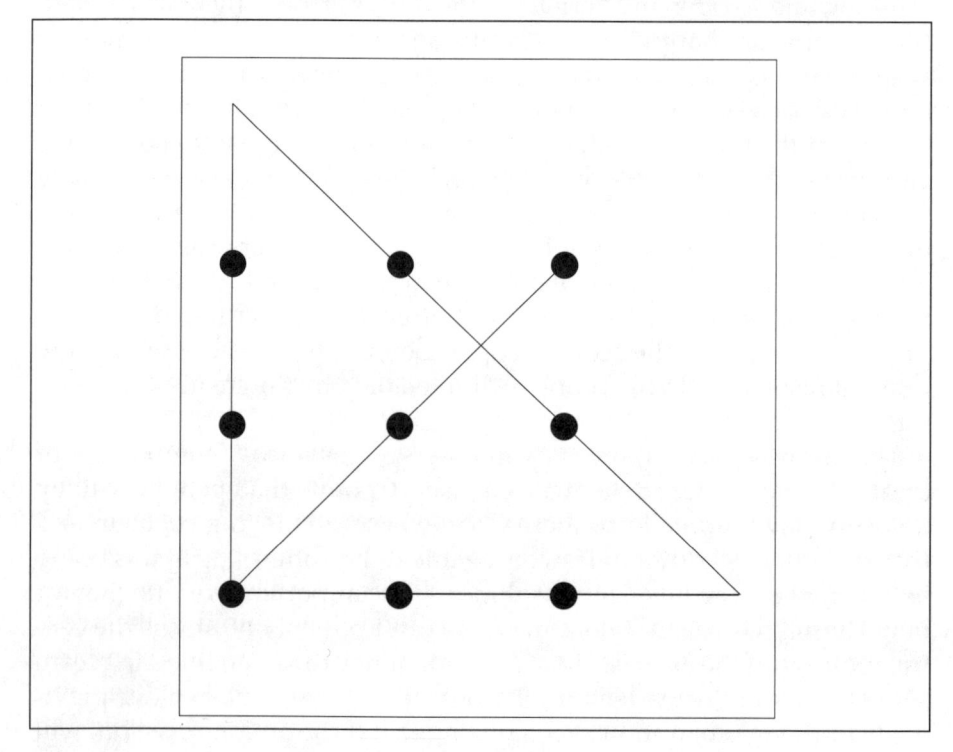

Figure 9.2 Solution to the nine-dot problem

importance of recognizing the artificial boundaries and constraints that we place around problems. In fact there are many solutions to this problem, all of which require creative thought. The one we like best was produced by a young girl who took a thick pencil and drew a line through all the dots. It is only by thinking 'out of the box' that we can solve many long-standing problems. For example, it was only by asking questions such as 'why does one job have to be performed by only one person?' and 'why do we have to work from nine to five?' that creative alternatives such as job sharing and flexitime were introduced. In re-engineering, teams need to question the 'constraints' that currently limit the way work is carried out within business processes.

Sometimes these constraints are so pervasive and so central to the way people think about work that they become invisible. Like the fish that is unaware its environment is wet, people become oblivious to their surroundings after a while and fail to recognize there are alternatives. The role of an external facilitator is important here in helping the team to 'see the wood from the trees' and asking questions like, 'what would happen if you just stopped doing that?'

Preparing the re-engineering team for this type of creative thinking is a necessary step in forming the right kind of environment where such thinking can flourish and where the team understands the full nature of the task that lies ahead. Once this has been done there are several techniques that can facilitate the development of new ideas, based on tried and tested problem-solving tools. Before we describe these, however, we will outline the role of 'process enablers': devices which enable new process designs through the innovative use of technological and human resources.

PROCESS ENABLERS

Designing a new process requires more than a creative imagination. The new process must be technologically possible if it is to replace the old, and it must achieve this in a way that makes sound economic sense. The benefits of a new process design in terms of meeting customer requirements or reducing lead times can only be feasible if the cost of achieving this does not outweigh the advantages. Achieving a balance between technical and economic viability is therefore a critical lever in process re-engineering. However, as many organizations have found to their cost, the technical superiority of a new process does not ensure it is translated into improved performance statistics. New processes must be acceptable in social and human terms if the new process is to work smoothly and achieve all that it is capable of. We will discuss the implications of this for managing the change to new processes in a later chapter. Here we will simply outline the importance of technical and human systems in enabling new processes to be designed.

THE ENABLING ROLE OF INFORMATION TECHNOLOGY

One of the reasons behind the development of BPR as a strategic business tool is the increasing use of new technology in virtually every aspect of an organization's operations, and the increasing power and capability of that technology. Technology enables new ways of working, and thus can spawn new process designs. The link is not an inevitable one, however. Computers have been a part of everyday business operations for over thirty years, and yet, even today, there are more examples of technology fitting within existing processes than of new processes being created from technology. Tasks such as producing a written document are performed differently now, using word processors rather than typewriters, carbon paper and lots of correction fluid, but the main steps in a process of which this may be one small part remain largely the same. In this respect, new technology has been used mainly to automate a process rather than to change it. The fears in the 1970s that new technology would lead to massive job losses have until recently remained unfounded because of this fact.

Automating a step in a process means it no longer has to be performed manually, though of course the step itself still remains. A secretary may use a spellcheck program rather than proofread a document, but the step of checking for typographical errors still remains. Similarly, the early introduction of new technology into manufacturing processes meant that tasks such as operating machine tools could be performed with absolute precision time after time using computer numerically controlled lathes, but the actual task of cutting material to specifications remained and continued to be performed by the machine operator, even though extensive deskilling resulted.

Although we usually think of new technology as allowing us to perform tasks like this with reliability and accuracy, there are a number of other ways in which it can be used, other than to automate steps in a process. For example, the *sequence* in which steps are performed can be altered using real-time links between computer workstations, particularly in the case of new product development. Thus the Boeing 777 was designed and constructed using concurrent engineering, where different parts were designed simultaneously, safe in the knowledge that everything would ultimately 'fit together' perfectly.

Computers can also be used as *analytical* tools, where processing power is harnessed to perform calculations, analyse data and aid decision-making. In these instances it is not so much a manual task that is replaced but an intellectual one. Another use is in *tracking*, where bar codes allow items to be logged and tracked as they are transported. This may simply reflect the sale of goods in a supermarket, though satellite systems now allow goods that are sent around the world or across continents to be tracked more or less continuously on their journey. New technology can also play a *de-mediator* role, whereby the people that normally mediate between parties in a process are replaced through a direct computer link being established. Virtual shopping malls on the Internet are now a reality in Britain, removing the link a retailer has traditionally played between manufacturer and purchaser.

If a process is to be changed in the radical and creative ways we have suggested, it can often be achieved only through the use of new technology in ways like these rather than through automating. In this respect, technology becomes an 'enabler' of process redesign, driving forward previously undreamt of ways of working. It helps enormously if the re-engineering team knows what is capable of being achieved with new technology. The team can then use this knowledge to 'break the rules' governing existing work practices. In some ways such action requires a new way of thinking about problems, based on inductive thinking rather than deductive thinking. Early writings on BPR have referred to this as starting with a solution and looking for a problem that it can solve, rather than deducing a solution from an existing problem.

The re-engineering team therefore needs to have a working knowledge of the technology that is available and the ways it can be used to change processes. Some of the more common ways are listed below, though the expanding use and development of emerging technologies means that this list should be constantly updated.

Electronic Data Interchange (EDI)

EDI systems allow data to be shared by using databases that can be accessed by several parties. They enable communication between parties via this direct computer link, thereby dispensing with written or telephone communications. Many internal departments are now linked in this way, enabling several steps within a process to be dispensed with. For example, a finance department can place all relevant financial and budgetary data on a database that can be accessed by individual departments as and when they need it. As a result the need for departments to request information and for the finance department to respond by extracting and conveying the information no longer exists. More radical process redesigns have allowed manufacturing companies to place their production schedules on such a database, with an EDI link to their external suppliers. The suppliers can consult these schedules and supply goods when the customer needs them without the customer even having to place an order.

Expert systems

An expert system is usually a menu-driven system of instructions that guides the user through a complex task. Based on the knowledge, heuristics and techniques used by experts in a particular field to solve problems and make decisions, expert systems allow non-experts to perform the same tasks by mimicking the specialist. Members of the public may come into contact with an expert system when registering for social security benefits that are based on complex formulas, or when consulting their doctor, who feeds information on their symptoms into a computer and is given a diagnosis and course of treatment by the system. Their key role in process re-engineering is in enabling non-experts and generalists to replace experts and specialists, thereby removing people from the process, which in turn means there can be fewer handovers between people, resulting in fewer delays or errors. Direct line insurance companies have transformed the process of taking out an insurance policy by enabling the majority of the process to be conducted over the telephone and removing the need for specialists to make decisions based on risk and personal circumstances.

Network links

Links between remote sites and a central base via computerized electronic mail and network software allow people to send and receive data. Paper-based systems are no longer required, and so time is saved in terms of printing and transportation tasks. Such links go much further than this, and enable people to have access to virtually all office-based systems from a remote location. In practical everyday terms many people can now perform many work duties from home, saving large amounts of time that may have been spent travelling to and from a central office. Such applications of this technology have obvious benefits but do not alter the processes that are used to produce the work required. More imaginative applications entail downloading office systems, so that the remote user performs more steps in a process instead of simply e-mailing their work to someone in an office for that person to perform their part in the process. In our own organization, consultants operating from their home base can design course materials using sophisticated desktop publishing packages and then e-mail the product to a central office for laser and colour printing. This new process has replaced the old method which involved a consultant conveying ideas for text, graphics and layout to a specialist who would then convert these ideas to a product which in turn would be reviewed by the consultant before printing could take place.

For organizations that have multiple sites, even if located across the globe, network links can provide a forum for information to be shared. Geographically diverse organizations can thereby achieve many of the benefits of team-based work and the sharing of ideas and experiences across members of teams, while at the same time being close to the customer. In some organizations this has not only changed the way key tasks and processes are performed, it has transformed the way in which the entire organization is structured, enabling decentralization to occur without losing the benefits of centrally co-ordinated processes. For example, purchasing decisions can be made locally, while still reaping the benefits of central purchasing, such as bulk order discounts.

Decision analysis systems

Making important decisions based on events that have not yet occurred is a fact of modern organizational life. Whether it involves ordering stock, introducing a new product to the market, investing in shares, or selling stock, decision-makers often feel they are having to operate 'blind'. Decision analysis systems allow a number of possible 'what if' scenarios to be created and optimum decision points and actions to be identified. While harnessing the analytical capabilities of software systems, enabling more effective decisions to be made, the benefit of these systems for process re-engineering comes when they are used to devolve decision-making to lower levels within the organizational hierarchy. Traditionally, making decisions has been the prerogative of management, which has led to jobs and processes being designed where approvals, authorizations and checks are built in to most processes. When they involve written requests and authorizations, as they most usually do, then a simple job can become paralysed with bureaucracy and the inevitable delays. By providing information and the tools to analyse it intelligently, these systems remove the need for decision-making to be made by management and enable it to be transferred to those charged with implementing the decisions. Decision analysis systems reduce the steps and delays in a process, without compromising the quality of the decisions that are made.

HUMAN RESOURCE ENABLERS

While the impetus for most process re-engineering has come from the world of information technology, through its enabling role, we should not overlook the role of human systems. There are now many ways of utilizing human resources over and above the simple exchange relationship based on financial remuneration. Without a knowledge of these systems and what they can enable, a team cannot achieve the full potential for process re-engineering, just as if it failed to consider the technological enablers outlined above.

Traditionally, human resources were ignored in the design of processes and technologies. One of the legacies of Frederick Taylor was that people were viewed as little more than machines, to be directed and controlled at the whim of management. Although it may seem like stating the obvious today, the findings from the studies of Elton Mayo at the Hawthorne plant of the Western Electric Company showed that the feelings and motivations of workers affected their productivity and performance. It is difficult to recognize today the revolutionary nature of such a conclusion. Yet there is still an after effect from this era, manifested in the way that until recently very little attention was paid to the management of human resources.

The introduction of Japanese management techniques in recent years shows how attitudes have gradually changed. Practices such as lifetime employment, seniority systems based on job rotation, and participative management are now seen as necessary to the success of a business, enabling the achievement of superior product and service quality and flexible work practices. As with information technology, the true value of these systems is realized when they are used as levers for process change and not just as 'modern management techniques'. We will therefore describe some of the human resource enablers and the ways they can be used to change business processes.

Autonomous work teams

Many work processes still involve individuals performing well-defined and specific tasks in much the same way as the production lines first designed by Henry Ford. Each individual forms a link in a chain of activities that eventually results in a finished product or service for the customer of that process. A large amount of research has shown that people who perform highly routinized and repetitive work experience job dissatisfaction, alienation from their work and even more general forms of poor mental health.

Autonomous work teams are a reaction against this form of work and are self-managed teams where each member is responsible for a whole task or complete job. This way each person sees the finished product of their labour, an essential form of feedback if they are to feel any sort of motivation for the job they perform. Such teams also take on most of the planning and decision-making responsibilities that traditionally are performed by managers. Thus the team may be responsible for allocating jobs among themselves, setting and achieving production targets, recording and responding to production data, solving quality problems, ordering supplies and even delivering finished goods to customers, be they internal or external.

In the jargon of BPR such teams are called 'case teams', though the term rather than the technique is the new phenomenon: this form of team-based work was developed in the 1970s, following pioneering work by behavioural scientists on how to design jobs in ways that maximized performance and job satisfaction. With such teams, processes that previously consisted of numerous hand-overs between individuals, often situated in different departments in different locations, are transformed to become a single set of activities performed by either one individual within the team or by the team itself.

The result has several advantages over the previous design. First, it drastically reduces the time taken to perform the process; because there are few if any hand-overs, delays between these are virtually eliminated. Second, it reduces the time spent checking on the progress of a job in response to customer requests; since all steps are now performed in a single team it takes much less time to find where a particular job is and how it is progressing. Third, it enhances the nature of work performed by individuals, through providing them with a greater sense of the whole task, closeness to the customer and more involvement in decision-making.

Autonomous work teams therefore enable jobs to be designed around the tasks involved, changing the nature of some of these tasks and in some cases removing them. As with technology enablers, the re-engineering team can start from the premiss of having this enabler available, and design the new process to make use of it.

Lifetime employment

The principle of guaranteeing an employee's job for life is one that is associated with Japanese organizations, and has had little impact on Western management. Nevertheless it enjoys a significant amount of interest in terms of its ability to achieve flexibility within a workforce, and can be a useful enabler of new process designs.

In fact only about one-third of the Japanese workforce work for the same employer throughout their working life. This guarantee often can be achieved only if a substantial amount of work is subcontracted, meaning that the guarantee is achieved by the very lack of long-term security afforded to others.

Despite these misconceptions, the principle is one that can be used as a powerful lever for change. Usually, this is through removing the obstacles that have previously prevented new ways of working rather than directly enabling a new design *per se*. Thus the Rover motor company was able to remove some of the traditional demarcations that prevented workers from performing jobs other than those that were explicitly recognized by their union by offering this type of guarantee in return for greater flexibility. This flexibility may mean that employees perform a wider array of jobs, and thus become 'case workers' within teams like those described above. It may also mean that the development path of managers within an organization encompasses routine 'shop floor' jobs, as is practised by some Japanese companies. This in turn may be used to enable new processes where managers perform some of the tasks traditionally performed by staff.

The concept of lifetime employment may be modified to something less than a guarantee for life while at the same time enabling some of the flexibility that it is intended to create. One organization we assisted with a large re-engineering project, wanted to involve senior and middle managers in the design of new processes, but recognized that these people were unlikely to re-engineer themselves out of a job. They resolved the difficulty by guaranteeing there would be no job losses as a result of process changes. We facilitated each of the teams and ensured the attention was on processes not jobs, and it was only after the new designs and structures were created that the Board then looked at ways of fitting managers to the new roles that had been created or placing them in other parts of the business where they could add real value. Although some people did not relish being moved to new jobs, the situation was not unlike that which accompanies lifetime employment and the flexibility that it necessitates.

Career planning

By concentrating on processes not functions, traditional vertical career paths can become things of the past. A true process orientation within an organization can reduce the number of options for upward advancement, leaving lateral development the only viable option. Once again such development can introduce barriers to radical change and a genuine process orientation. By developing new career paths that are linked to processes, an organization can remove these barriers and enable the new designs to be implemented in a way that will motivate rather than alienate those that operate them. One technique that can help here is that of technical career paths. Usually, progression up the organizational hierarchy means taking on more managerial responsibility and less technical responsibility. Technically competent individuals are often faced with a choice of relinquishing their greatest strengths in favour of career progression, or forgoing progression in order to continue exercising their technical skills. A different career path, based on increasing a person's responsibility for the development of technical aspects of the process while reducing managerial responsibilities avoids this type of choice and can act as a motivator for those involved.

We were able to introduce this type of enabler within a software development company, where difficulties were being experienced among the management team. Although most of the team had risen up the organizational hierarchy based on their technical skills, most had been prepared to take on increasing managerial responsibility in return for promotion, even though this took them away from the technical aspects of the job. However, two members of the team were distinctly uncomfortable in this type of role, and performed it poorly. The situation became acute when the team began to develop the role of process owner, where the need to manage and influence people across functions without any formal authority over them became an additional requirement of every member of the team. The team faced a number of difficult choices. It could demote these two individuals to their former roles, though neither the team nor the individuals wanted this. Or it could put them through a developmental programme aimed at increasing their managerial and leadership skills, with the possibility that this might not reap significant benefits given their reluctance to apply these skills.

The answer came when we suggested that the team created a new role that played to the team's strengths rather than its weaknesses. The two individuals concerned disliked having to manage people, so this responsibility was removed, along with the traditional accoutrements of this role which also caused them discomfort (specifically, having to dress like a manager). They were not required to participate in the team's decision-making and strategy formulation, unless they explicitly wanted to do so on specific issues. Instead their time was spent either in a small office where they were unlikely to be interrupted by staff, or working from home. Their new role involved solving technical problems and developing the IT enablers that would drive new process designs. It represented an advancement on their earlier technical roles and skills, in that its aim was more strategic, while avoiding the managerial responsibilities that had until then prevented the development of such a role among senior managers.

Although most members of the management team were not attracted by this alternative career development path, it provided a suitable goal for those in the team below who were attracted by it, and who until that time had faced a choice between advancement or technical specialization. The new career path enabled the organization to move towards a new structure and management hierarchy based on lateral processes without having to fit this within a career structure based on upward advancement.

360° appraisals

In process-oriented teams, performance management should reflect a team-based rather than individual-based approach. One of the best ways of doing this is through the use of 360° appraisals. These provide performance feedback to an individual from three directional sources: downwards, from the person's boss; laterally, from his or her peers, and upwards, from their subordinates. The addition of two directional sources has two distinct advantages over the traditional downward appraisal that is involved in most performance management systems. First, lateral appraisal encompasses more than the usual concerns of a person's manager. Peers within the team will have particular requirements of each other, and this demands a relationship where performance goals can be negotiated without formal authority over one another. The skills required of each individual to do this are likely to be somewhat different from those where authority is formalized through a hierarchical relationship. Individuals therefore need feedback from their colleagues on how well they do this and whether they need to improve.

A second advantage of this system is that where such hierarchical relationships do exist, there is an additional requirement for an individual to be more of a coach than a manager. Because process teams involve their members in decision-making and concentrate their effort and skills on satisfying customers, the role of the traditional manager becomes extinct. Since tasks will have been combined into single jobs performed by one person, there is less need for managers to check on the progress of work as it moves from task to task and person to person. Monitoring and controlling should become duties of the past under this kind of set-up. The new requirement is a manager who is able to develop a high-level of autonomy among his or her team while at the same time not feeling threatened by this. The use of upward appraisal creates this type of relationship between a manager and his or her subordinates, since it challenges the very principles of the formal relationship between both parties, allowing the subordinate to influence the behaviour of the manager through giving him or her feedback on their performance.

Such appraisal systems are key enablers of processes that make use of autonomous work teams and which push decision-making responsibilities down the organizational hierarchy to where the work is performed. They facilitate the flow of communication both laterally and upwardly, providing teams with the oxygen of information required for superior team, individual and process performance.

Organizational and management development

Our experience of working with organizations managing large-scale change has confirmed time after time the importance of integrating organizational development and management development. The sociotechnical systems school founded by the Tavistock Institute of Human Relations during the 1950s and 1960s first demonstrated the need to take into account the social aspects of a system as well as the technical aspects. Technologically driven changes in the design of a job would not achieve their full potential if the human and social implications of the change were not recognized and managed accordingly. Little has altered since that time, and changes in process design brought about by the enabling role of new technologies must be accompanied by changes in human resource policies of the kind outlined above if they are to realize their full potential.

Armed with their knowledge of IT and HR enablers, the re-engineering team is thus ready to take its first bold steps in re-engineering the process that has been selected. Although these steps will be driven by this knowledge and the process vision, there is still a need for some general principles that will assist the team in creating the new process. We will consider now the practical application of these principles.

10 Principles

The design of the new process is likely to be developed over the course of several weeks by the re-engineering team. During that time the team will explore several options, gather relevant data and information and make adjustments where necessary. Even after the design has been provisionally agreed, the task of developing the key enablers may mean the team has to make further changes to the design of the new process. In re-engineering the process, the team should draw upon the preparatory work it has done on determining customer requirements, benchmarking and visioning, as well as its knowledge of human and technological enablers. The team should also draw upon a number of principles or guidelines that can help it in the task of creating a new process design. Some of these principles have their origins in the school of Operations and Management, developed to help people design jobs that maximized efficiency. Others are new, and capture the radicalism that distinguishes BPR from these earlier approaches to business improvement. It is to these principles that we now turn.

In putting the principles into practice, the re-engineering team should attempt to use them creatively. Hence a technique based on brainstorming should be used to achieve this. We will say more on this issue later. The team should also remember that these are principles not imperatives. There will be cases where it is not wise to apply them, given other factors and constraints. 'Honesty is the best policy' is a principle most people can accept and aim to fulfil, while still recognizing that there may be times when it is not prudent to be entirely truthful. The re-engineering teams should treat these principles of re-engineering in a similar way.

PRINCIPLES OF RE-ENGINEERING

There are six main principles for BPR, each of which is discussed below.

AS FEW PEOPLE AS POSSIBLE SHOULD BE INVOLVED IN THE PROCESS

The re-engineering team should attempt to remove as many people as possible from involvement in performing the tasks that make up the process. This can be done by combining tasks so that any one person performs more steps within the process. One of the legacies of Taylorism is specialization, with complex jobs being fragmented into specific parts that are then performed by a range of specialists. Process re-engineering involves challenging this approach, and replacing specialists with generalists who are able to perform a greater range of jobs. Thus rather than have six people perform six steps within a process, two people might perform three steps each. It is usually not too difficult to see how this can be done within departments, but the true challenge for the re-engineering team is to remove people that are in different functions, resulting in entire departments being left out of a process. This is difficult because these functions have specialized roles to play within a process. An accounting department performs financial transactions, while a production department is involved in the construction of a physical product. To combine tasks would therefore mean that people are performing duties which they have not previously been trained or expected to perform, and which traditionally have been performed by specialists in other departments. Many teams would not even consider such changes, since they are adverse to how we normally view work. Yet re-engineering involves this type of challenge to the common orthodoxy and the role of the re-engineering team is to look at such radical alternatives, since it is through changes of this kind that great improvements can be made in terms of the time taken to perform the process.

Proposing that someone in one specialist department should perform the duties of someone in another is the kind of creative thinking outlined in the previous chapter. Yet it is hardly pragmatic, and the team may be left with the feeling that although such ideas may be creative they are unlikely to be of much practical use. If so, the team needs to consider what is necessary to enable such a change in the process, giving attention to the IT and HR enablers outlined in Chapter 9. For example, an expert system can enable specialist tasks requiring expert knowledge to be performed by people with little background or training in that specialism. This is one way of combining specialist roles into one job, creating a generalist or multiskilled individual where collections of specialists once existed.

This kind of approach characterizes the difference between BPR and earlier approaches that resulted in less dramatic improvements in the performance of processes. In the past such creative ideas were unlikely to have been raised, and even if they were, the most common response was to laugh them off as crazy ideas with little or no practical application. In BPR the response is to find ways of enabling these ideas to be implemented by using the technological and human resources that are now available.

This kind of approach was used in our work with an IT department within a financial services company. One of this department's roles was to purchase and install PCs for users in other parts of the business. Only a few years previously, having a PC on one's desk was the privilege of managers only, and the IT department was able to cope easily with the occasional request to have one bought and installed. Over the years however, virtually every staff member with a desk had a PC on it, and the process failed to keep pace with this exponential increase in demand. The problems experienced illustrated the inadequacy of a process designed under entirely different conditions: primarily the process was lengthy, with users having to wait up to three months to obtain a new PC. Their expectations of what they would receive were often quite different from what was actually installed, resulting in frustration and dissatisfaction. The responsibilities and accountabilities of those people involved in the process were not clearly defined, and so when a user complained the complaint was passed 'from pillar to post' with no one taking responsibility for errors or for putting matters right. Not only did users find the process complicated and confusing, members of the IT department were also unclear as to how the process should perform. On the whole, the process was ripe for re-engineering.

Unfortunately, the team that was set up to improve matters had little knowledge of process re-engineering, and had little desire to cause disruption with radical alternatives. Their approach was to improve the process largely by clarifying the steps involved in the process and the responsibilities of those required to perform them. Although the team claimed success from its work, it was clear to most people (especially users) that the problems had not been tackled. Within a short time it was still taking three months for some people to receive their computers. The IT department's Quality Co-ordinator asked if we could help, suggesting that it may be worth considering some of the more radical alternatives involved in process re-engineering.

Our first reaction when we looked at the process was that too many people were involved. Historically, as the requirements and expectations of users had become more sophisticated, more specialists had been added to the process to meet this demand. We produced a data flow diagram showing the main steps of the process and the people that carried them out: no fewer than ten distinct groups within the IT department were involved, and this did not include the steps performed by other departments such as finance, distribution, and goods inwards! The

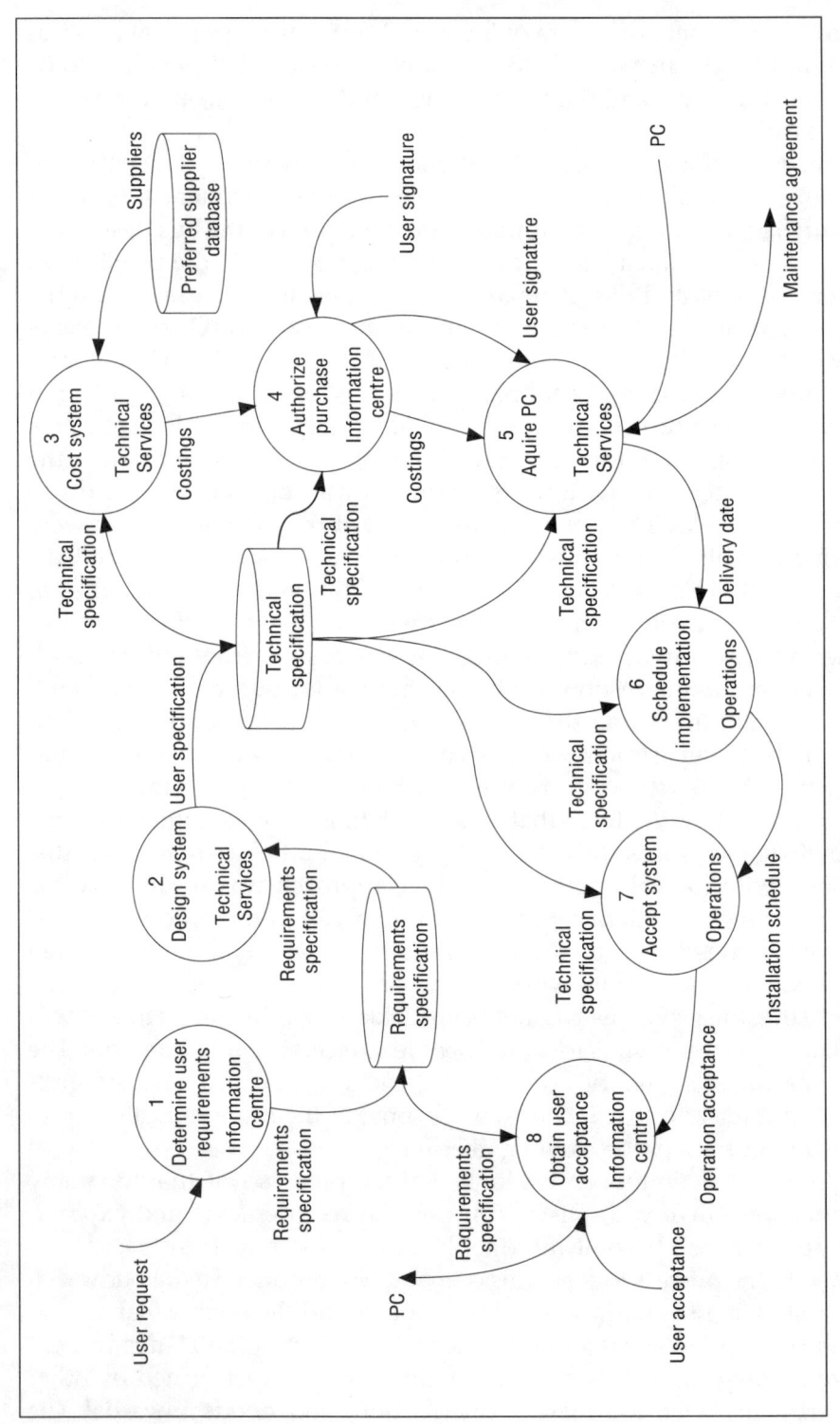

Figure 10.1 PC purchasing process

diagram is reproduced in Figure 10.1.

The key role within the process was that performed by the Technical Services group, yet even within this relatively specialized team distinct tasks like designing the system and costing it were performed by different individuals. Because so many other groups and individuals were involved, a considerable amount of time was spent by Technical Services producing a technical specification that would allow each of these parties to extract the information they needed. Yet if most of these steps could be performed by Technical Services there would be no need for them to produce such a detailed specification, since no one else would need this information. The main thrust of our approach was to apply the principle of as few people as possible being involved in the process, and this meant challenging the roles performed by others and whether these steps could either be omitted or performed by Technical Services.

Figure 10.1 shows that staff in the Information Centre had the closest contact with the customer, in terms of agreeing the original requirements at the beginning of the process and obtaining a sign-off at the end to state that these had been met, yet they had little involvement in the intervening steps other than to authorize the purchase. This meant that they were often caught in the middle of disputes over changes in requirements, sometimes negotiating these changes with their IT colleagues and on other occasions explaining to customers why the changes had not been incorporated. When pressed, the Quality Co-ordinator was unable to say why Technical Services could not determine the user's requirements, other than that this task had always been performed by the Information Centre. The skills involved were by no means confined to the latter, and in most respects Technical Services would be better placed to advise the user on the implications of their requirements.

Similarly, the involvement of Operations was largely administrative, scheduling the implementation, other than when they arranged the technical acceptance of the new PC by the existing operating system. Since this made use of the technical data produced by Technical Services, this task could easily be performed by the latter. By progressively removing steps from the process (authorization was only required for purchases that were particularly expensive and outside the range of the usual type of request) and combining others into the role of Technical Services, we were able to remove virtually every other party from this process. The new process could be represented by the data flow diagram shown in Figure 10.2.

Since there were no handovers between groups within the IT department, the average time to perform the process was reduced from four weeks to one week. Customers dealt only with Technical Services, and

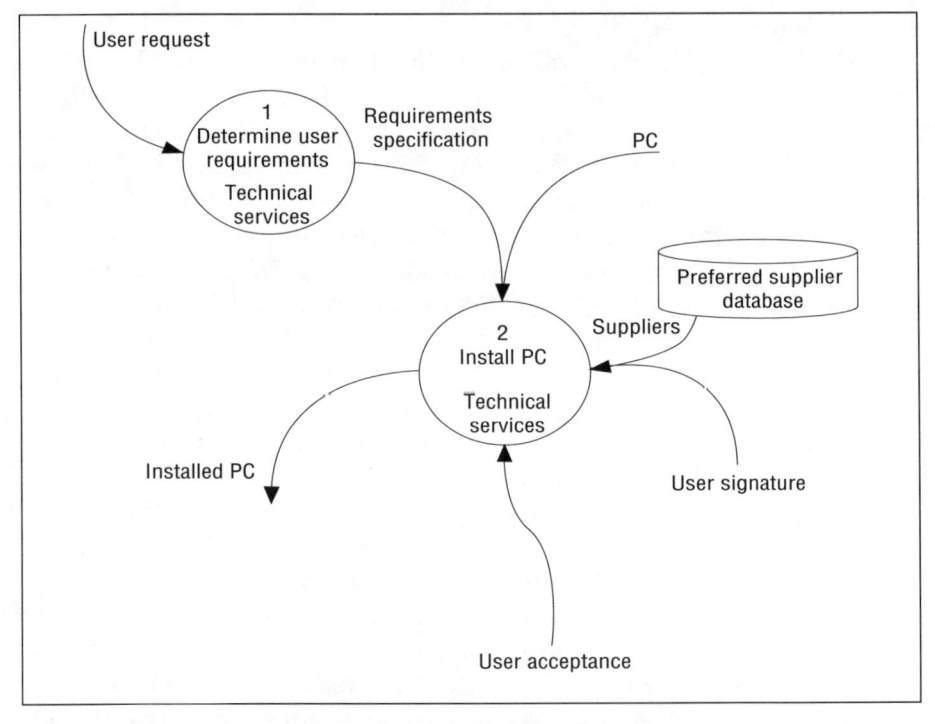

Figure 10.2 Re-engineered PC installation process

so did not have to spend time tracking down the person who was dealing with the request at the time that any problems were experienced. Responsibilities and accountabilities could not have been clearer, and this meant that there was no need for the authorizations and sign-offs at various stages, which had only existed to protect the various parties from customer complaints.

The changes that were made to the process combined tasks and removed the number of people within a process. The alert reader may have noticed, however, that the changes were all made within the IT department and that this was just one sub-process of a larger process involving the customer's department, finance, and goods inwards. A higher-level data flow diagram would show these departments and the linkages between them, and it would have been possible to re-engineer the process on this scale. Since the changes we recommended were initially greeted with some incredulity by the IT management it is most unlikely that the organization was ready for change on this larger scale! Nevertheless such changes were theoretically possible, and would have incorporated some of the additional principles other than this one.

THE CUSTOMERS OF A PROCESS SHOULD PERFORM THAT PROCESS

This principle is similar to the first, in that it achieves gains in process performance largely through reducing the number of people involved in the process. It is helpful because it offers some guidance as to who should perform the tasks that are combined into single roles. Most processes involve people or departments that are linked by internal customer-supplier relationships. One department produces goods or services that are used by another department, making it the first department's customer. In Total Quality Management (TQM), improvements are made by ensuring the internal supplier has agreed the requirements of its internal customer and meets those requirements 'right first time'. Through the principle described here, BPR attempts something far more radical: remove the supplier and have the customer do the job.

The scope for introducing this principle can be gauged from the data flow diagrams that the re-engineering team will have produced. Processes or sub-processes that start with a request, pass through several departments or individuals, and end with an output that goes back to the party making the request should be identified and the team should ask whether the receiving customer could have performed many if not all of the intervening steps. In the above example drawn from an IT department, Figure 10.1 shows that the Information Centre is the end customer of the sub-process that exists within the department. One alternative design to that of having Technical Services perform all the steps would have been for the Information Centre to have done this. In fact we did consider this option, though it would have meant the development of a more powerful enabler – an expert system allowing the Information Centre to perform all the technical tasks previously performed by Technical Services and Operations.

Of course, this principle can be applied in even more radical ways. The true customer of the PC ordering process was the user, someone outside the IT department and with few or none of their technical skills. To have involved this person in performing the process could have produced additional savings in time but would probably have demanded more effective process enablers. Yet more and more companies are adopting such an approach to internal purchasing, and achieve it through providing their staff with corporate-style credit cards that allow them to purchase goods directly from external suppliers. Indeed, one of the comments often made by staff having to wait three months to have a PC installed was, 'I could have bought one myself from the High Street and avoided all this delay'.

How the principle can be applied to external customers was demon-

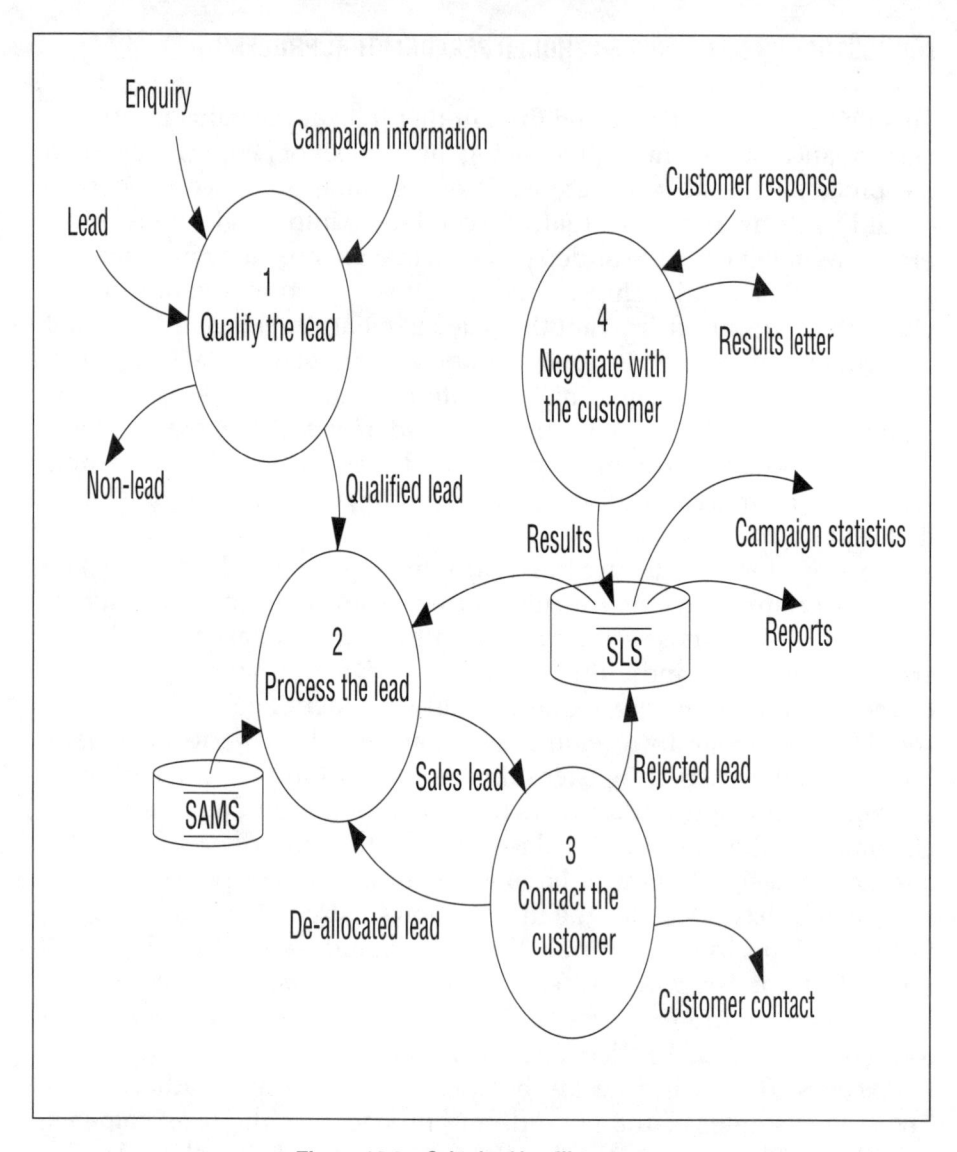

Figure 10.3 Sales lead handling process

strated by one of our clients in the telecommunications industry. Their sales lead handling process was taking too long to feed leads through to the sales team, taking up to eight weeks after the original customer enquiry with the result that many leads were lost through becoming 'cold'. After such a long wait to have their call returned, most customers had understandably taken their business elsewhere. Inevitably there were recriminations between salespeople and those whose job it was to qualify and filter the leads to them (*see* Figure 10.3 for a data flow diagram of the process).

In creating their vision of the new process, the re-engineering team appointed to improve the situation established a truly bold concept. Rather than just reduce the process time, they proposed to perform the whole process in real time. Everyone knew that a sales lead was at its 'hottest' when the customer was actually on the telephone making the enquiry, yet this simple fact had become lost in the bureaucracy that had been built up to qualify, process and allocate the lead. What was needed was a process that could qualify and feed a lead through to a salesperson while the customer was making the call.

In considering how it might apply the principle of customers performing parts of the process, someone in the team suggested that customers could qualify their own leads. He did not know how this could be done and at first sight it seemed a rather silly suggestion. However, closer examination of this sub-process showed that it largely involved an operator asking the customer a series of standard questions. The next step was to see if there was a human or technological enabler that would allow customers to filter their own enquiry. The technology required to do this was an Automated Call Distributor (ACD): a recorded message that asks telephone callers to key in numbers from their phone pad according to the service they require. By using the criteria for separating genuine sales leads from other types of enquiries, callers were indeed able to qualify their own lead. A second enabler was an EDI link between salespeople and the database used to allocate these leads so that the internal customer of the process (the salesperson) was also performing part of the process, a further application of the principle. These changes meant that salespeople could speak directly to the caller, negotiating a deal there and then.

Some calls did not require the involvement of a salesperson: the customer simply wanted to place an order. In the past this type of call would follow the route of a standard enquiry, resulting in a call back from the salesperson several weeks later, usually after the customer had bought from a competitor. But filtering these calls through the ACD to the operators, an immediate sale could be made, which left the sales team free to respond to those enquiries that were less clear-cut and where their skills in selling were required.

A further benefit of the re-engineering process was that one of the databases used to support the old process could be virtually dispensed with – a cost saving to the company of £ million. Not only was the company saving such a large amount of money, it was making money by translating more enquiries into sales. Sales staff were receiving larger bonuses since less of their time was spent following up leads that had long since gone cold, and the operators also received bonuses for the sales that they made. It was a win/win outcome for all concerned.

The principle is not a new one. As customers of goods and services from buying petrol to making wills, people are now more prepared to perform parts of processes that were previously performed by 'specialists'. Most managers perform routine word-processing tasks that previously their secretaries performed. The principle does not imply that every step of the process is carried out by the customer or that customer does this for every transaction. But it does mean that where possible the customer is involved in the process to a far greater extent than traditionally has been the case. The importance of knowing the internal customer's requirements and of meeting these requirements, one of the foundations of the TQM philosophy, becomes redundant through the application of this principle. In fact it only became important to meet customer requirements because jobs were fragmented into internal customer-supplier roles in the first place.

TREAT SUPPLIERS AS THOUGH THEY ARE PART OF THE ORGANIZATION

The corollary of the previous principle sometimes means that external suppliers are required to perform steps in the process that were previously carried out internally. Buying work-based PCs from a high street store doesn't remove the need for a technical specification, it simply means the supplier rather than an internal IT department has to glean this. The principle described here means that where possible the re-engineering team should look at ways of involving external suppliers in performing parts of the process. Some motor manufacturers have been able to eliminate vast parts of their purchasing processes by requiring their suppliers to decide when to replenish stocks. The technology used as the enabler of this new process is an EDI link between the production department and the supplier, allowing the latter to make the purchasing decisions that were previously made in-house. In return for taking on this extra responsibility, they are given preferred supplier status, resulting in a win/win outcome for both parties.

In effect, the barriers between organizations become blurred and are moved when this type of principle is applied. Figure 10.4 shows this application for a typical purchasing process, although it can be applied to other aspects of a business, such as warehousing and logistics. When applied to internal suppliers of goods or services, it results in the kind of changes that were made in the IT department referred to above, where Technical Services performed the tasks that their internal customer, Information Centre, had previously performed.

Many organizations have achieved benefits from applying this principle in such a way that it results in key parts of a process being outsourced to another organization. When applied in conjunction with the

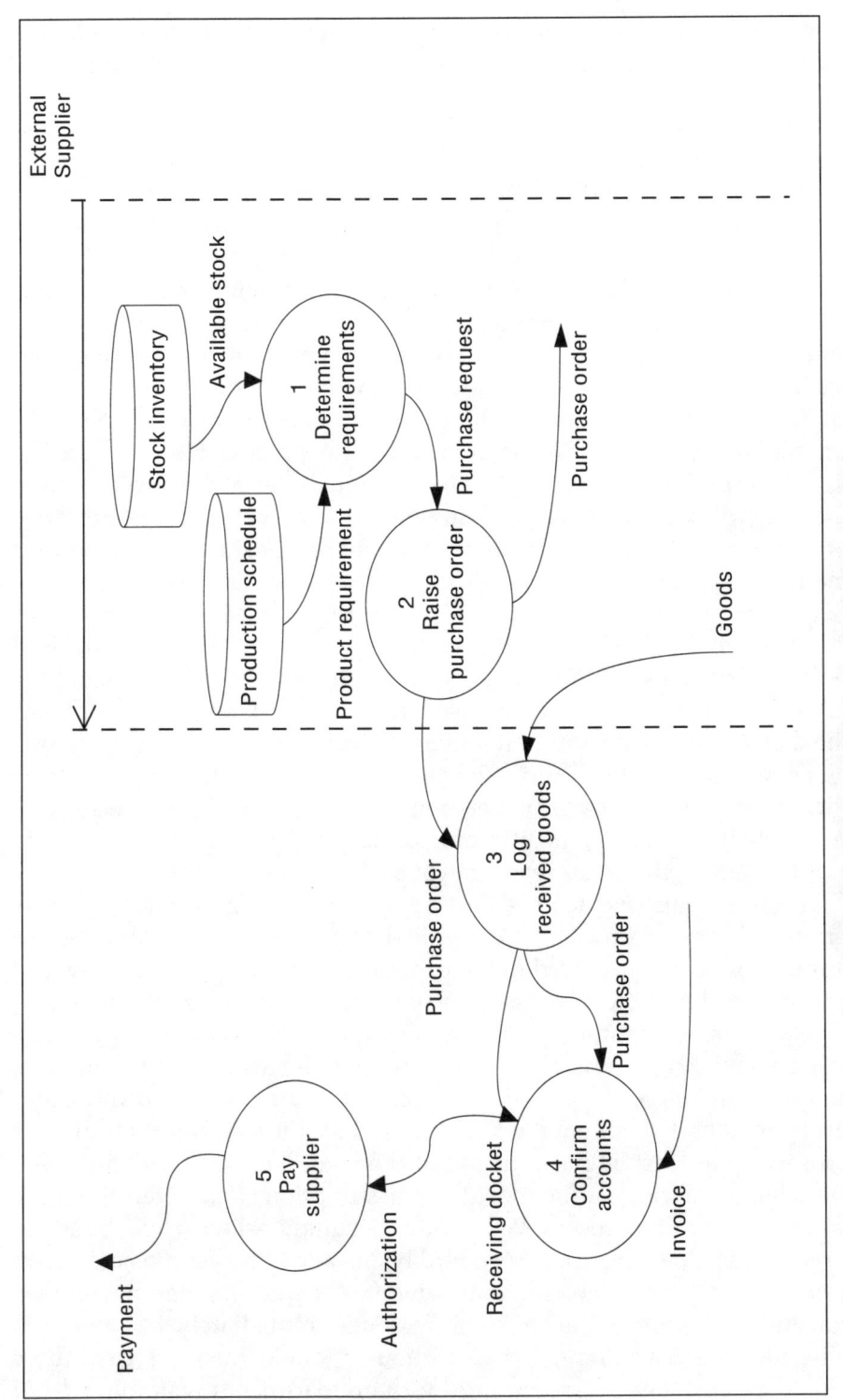

Figure 10.4 Changing role of suppliers in the purchasing process

previous two principles, we begin to get a sense of the scale of change that BPR can bring. A process consisting of four sub-processes spanning four main functions can be re-engineered into a process that has just one sub-process, with other sub-processes now being performed by customers and suppliers.

Change on this kind of scale was achieved by a re-engineering team we worked with in the finance sector. This team was created to examine the process of installing a Local Area Network (LAN) for business users, which was taking up to eight months to complete. There had been numerous attempts on previous occasions to improve the process, but any gains had been relatively short-lived, with the process reverting back to the *status quo* almost through a will of its own. Following re-engineering, the lead time of the process was cut to just four days, an unimaginable figure for those involved in the process. How was such a drastic improvement achieved? The case illustrates of the application of the principles that have been discussed so far, as well as the importance of creative thinking that challenges some of the most basic assumptions made by organizations.

The original process is shown in Figure 10.5. Most of the delays occurred in establishing the two business cases that were required before a decisions could be taken to order the equipment and install the LAN. Since both cases were required, the process always took as long as the slowest of these; any gains made in quickly putting together one business case were lost waiting for the second one to be completed. Thus there was little incentive for each department involved in these steps to complete their work in the minimum amount of time, which resulted in a downward spiral of the lead time of both sub-processes.

The re-engineering team's first attempt to re-engineer this process produced a new process that applied the principle of reducing the number of people involved in the process. Sub-processes 1 and 2 would be combined into one process, to be performed by one team. There was now a genuine incentive, driven by customer demands, to complete this stage as quickly as possible. Combining two departments into one was an unusually large step within this rather traditional organization, and the team felt satisfied that it was able to reduce the lead time of the entire process by at least 50 per cent. What the team had not done, however, was challenge some of the most basic assumptions that determined the parameters of this process. When our consultant asked why a business case was needed before a LAN could be installed, the team reacted with a mixture of puzzlement and amusement. The question had never been considered before, so an answer was not immediately obvious. On reflection the team agreed that without a sound business case there would be reckless overspending by the departments wanting a LAN

PRINCIPLES

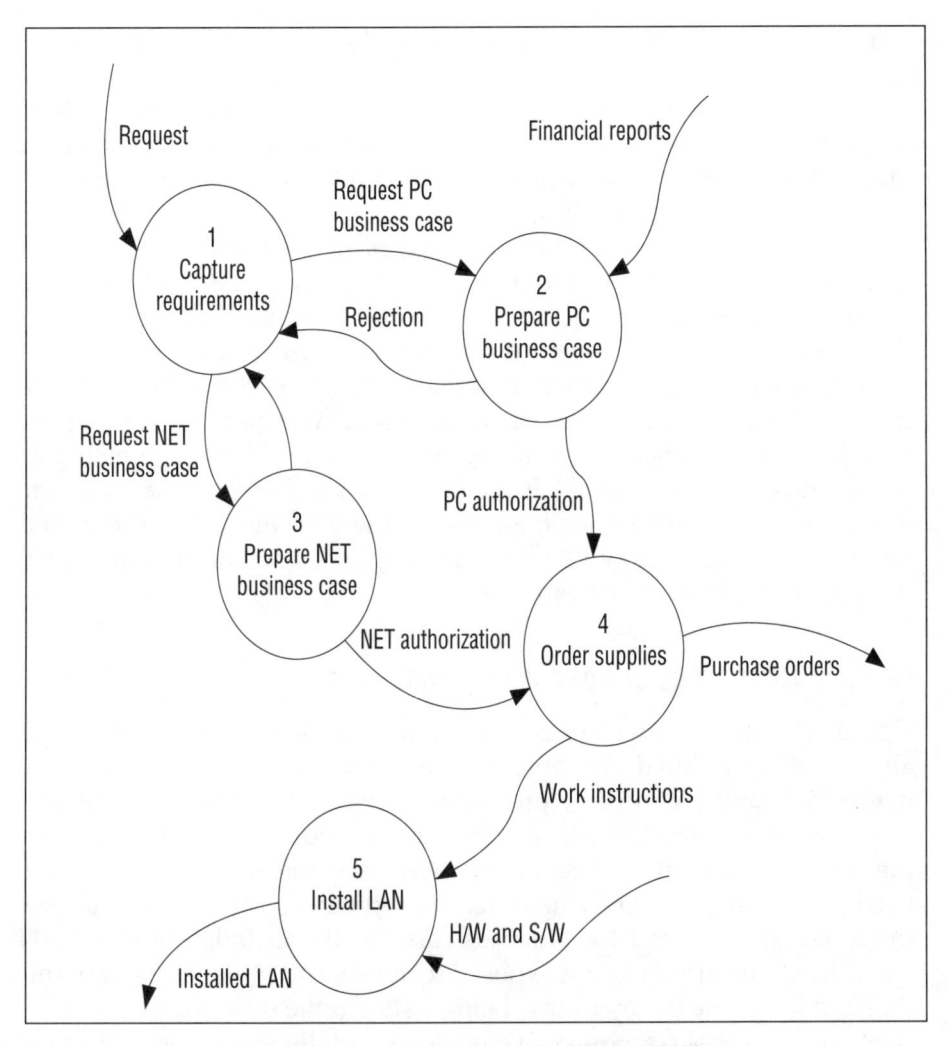

Figure 10.5 Installing a Local Area Network (LAN)

installed. However it soon became clear that departmental budgets would not allow this, and there was no real reason to suspect they would behave in such an unbusinesslike way.

Once this most basic of assumptions had been articulated and questioned, the team began to see other possibilities opening up before them. Most of the lead time of the process was taken up preparing the business cases. If these were omitted, the process of ordering supplies and installing the equipment could be performed in a matter of days following the initial request. Now the aim of the team became moving steps 4 and 5 closer in time to the original customer request. By applying the principle of treating suppliers as if they were part of the company, the team hit upon the idea of combining steps 1 and 4 and outsourcing these

133

to a supplier. In many ways suppliers were the best people to capture the user's requirements and match these with the appropriate hardware and software. The only step remaining in this process was step 5, which could be performed within one or two days of the original request being made. A process previously taking up to eight months to complete was therefore reduced to one taking no more than four days.

One of the requirements this particular principle highlights is trust in external suppliers. The traditional relationship with external suppliers is often an adversarial one, and it is clear that neither the LAN installation process nor any other processes that make use of this principle can operate unless there is implicit trust that suppliers will not provide more than what is actually needed. Trust can be achieved only if there is a genuine partnership with the supplier; we can think of this partnership as an additional enabler aimed at the organizational level rather than the technological or human level. Such a partnership needs to be founded on win/win outcomes, where both the supplier and the customer gain business benefits from the venture.

CREATE MULTIPLE VERSIONS OF COMPLEX PROCESSES

One of the keys to the kinds of changes that have been highlighted above is an additional principle that allows fundamental changes to be made while at the same time preserving some of the organizational controls that have been the basis for the original process. This is the principle of creating multiple versions of processes, some of which remove the need for controls, others which maintain them. In the example above, the removal of a need for business cases in the installation of a LAN could leave the organization exposed to abuse, and it was the fear of this that had led to the business case being a step in the process.

Many processes contain such controls, typically involving additional people, authorizations and inevitable delays, and are justified by reference to what might go wrong without them. At first sight these justifications appear perfectly sensible, but when they are examined more closely they are needed in only a small number of cases. One building society we worked with had a hugely complicated purchasing process with numerous authorizations and controls. When asked why the process was so complex the purchasing manager referred to an event some years earlier when an employee had attempted to swindle the company out of £150,000. The current process was designed to prevent that from occurring again, and appeared to be quite sensible against this background. Yet about three-quarters of all purchases were for less than £500, and many were for just a few pounds. Staff were exasperated at having to follow the same procedure to buy some stationery as when making a purchase for tens of thousands of pounds. In this case the possibility of what could go wrong without such controls only had the effect of preserving the controls in any attempt to change the process, and ultimately had kept the process in place against any attempt to improve it.

The key to this conundrum is to consider the parameters in which such controls make sense, and to create a separate process that operates within such controls, and additional processes that do not. Most insurance companies use this principle in dealing with claims. An assessor is needed to verify the claim if the company is to avoid fraudulent claims, yet this only makes economic sense for those that are over a certain value. The company therefore operates a process that includes assessment for claims above that amount and a more streamlined process without assessment for relatively small claims.

The idea of removing the need for a business case for LAN instalments in the case mentioned above was initially greeted with some disbelief and, as might be expected, this was supported with worst-case scenarios. Once we determined the proportion of requests such a worst case could occur in, it became apparent that most requests could proceed without a business case being required. A second process, with the two business cases being prepared by one team, was created for specialist requests where significant abuse of the system could occur or where the costs involved were significantly higher than average.

In a similar fashion, reducing the number of people involved in a process by combining tasks previously performed by specialists is often resisted by making reference to the complexity of the tasks. The need to maintain the specialists is justified by referring to tasks that couldn't possibly be performed by a generalist even with the help of an expert system. However, such cases usually account for only a small proportion of those handled by the process, and most of the specialist's time is spent on routine cases. The solution is to create two processes, one where generalists handle the majority of cases and one where specialists handle the small minority that need specialist skills and knowledge. When the telecommunications company re-engineered its sales lead handling process it actually created two processes, one which fed a potential buyer directly through to a salesperson, and another which fed a confirmed buyer through to an operator who was able to take the details and arrange the sale. Previously, salespeople had been dealing with both types of calls, even though their skills in negotiating sales were only required for the former type of call.

REDUCE THE NUMBER OF INPUTS INTO A PROCESS

A vast amount of time in many organizations is spent reconciling different accounts of the same thing. Holiday forms are matched with days on leave, purchase requests are matched with invoices received, patient records are matched with doctors' reports, airline tickets with bookings, and so on. The list is virtually endless. Processes that contain sub-processes and tasks involving such reconciliation are likely to be slow and cumbersome and require many people. Reducing the number of inputs into the process is one way of cutting down on the amount of reconciliation that is performed, speeding up the process and reducing headcount. The improvement is made simply by removing those inputs that have to be reconciled with others, although such a change may require an enabler or significant changes in other parts of the process.

The significance of this principle was highlighted in a simple but effective way for a team of maintenance engineers in a large educational institution. The team was meeting regularly to discuss a number of improvements in the way it responded to calls for maintenance work. One of the obstacles it was having to deal with was the large amount of paperwork supervisors had to deal with, keeping them away from the job of supervising the work of their tradespeople. At least one full day a week was spent matching the tradespeople's time sheets with the dockets giving job times. Although most conferred, the small minority that didn't confer accounted for most of the time taken to perform this task. Over the period of the team's work, the Estates department moved to new offices, and during the transition there was a period of a few weeks where both new and old offices were being used. The team leader had an office in both locations, and inevitably messages about the location of the meetings became garbled, resulting in some team members arriving at one office and the rest at the other. After this had happened on two or three occasions, someone pointed out that the problem had been created by the team leader having two offices, and that as soon as he got back to just one there would be little chance of it occurring again.

With this in mind our consultant suggested that the problem of time sheets failing to match job dockets was created by the fact that there were two records of how the tradespeople spent their time, and that if the time sheets were abolished then the supervisors would no longer have to reconcile them with job dockets. Although tradespeople had always kept time sheets, and this was seen as an important mechanism in controlling how they spent their time, no other employees had to account for their time hour by hour. In practice, the time sheets were little more than a sham, with tradespeople adjusting the recorded times to ensure they added up to an eight-hour shift. By dispensing with time sheets the three supervisors were able to save up to a full day each week on the amount of time spent on paperwork.

Data flow diagrams that show a number of inputs flowing into a sub-process highlight where bottlenecks are likely to occur due to excessive reconciliation. Removal of at least one of these inputs can save a significant amount of time. Some organizations have found that by introducing invoiceless purchasing processes they are able to reduce drastically the size of their accounts payable department, since much of the time spent by people in these departments involves reconciling information on invoices with that on purchase orders and receiving documents. Others have introduced bar-coding as an enabling technology that removes the need for goods to have separate paper records of their purchase or sale. As with any application of new technology in BPR, the principle of reducing inputs should be used to change a process and not just to automate it, therefore enabling the process to be performed in fewer steps and with fewer people, and is an effective way of achieving both.

MAINTAIN DECENTRALIZED UNITS WHILE CENTRALIZING COMMUNICATIONS

Although there are many advantages to decentralization, it can create problems. With processes that have several contact points with customers, and where customers are likely to make frequent enquiries about the progress of their request, a common problem is the difficulty of tracking down their order and the person dealing with it at the time of the enquiry. In our experience the usual response to this is to centralize key parts of the process. This might involve feeding all requests through one single point of order, or creating a centralized help desk to deal with all enquiries. In any event the advantages of decentralization are often lost through drawing people back into the centre and, paradoxically, further away from the customer.

Until recently, it was not possible to have the benefits of both centralization and decentralization. However, the use of technological enablers like EDI, shared databases, e-mail links and the virtual office mean that people and business units can remain decentralized while being able to communicate with each other and the customer as though they were centralized. Some of the ways in which this can be achieved were outlined in the previous chapter when the enabling technology was discussed. In applying the principle, teams need to use it as a way of maintaining current organizational structures or, in a positive way, as a means of creating new structures that increase decentralization to an extent that was previously resisted due to the lack of centralized control it might have implied.

APPLYING THE PRINCIPLES OF RE-ENGINEERING

The above principles show how a process can be re-engineered to produce forms of working that are dramatically different from the functionally based Tayloristic pattern of work that has dominated businesses and industry since the turn of the century. To use them effectively requires a combination of creative and analytical thinking from the re-engineering team. Creative thinking will generate ideas without the constraints that might inhibit their application in practice, while analytical thinking will aid the group in developing these ideas and key enablers as a way of making the process vision a reality.

To generate both types of thinking processes we have found it useful to usevarious problem-solving techniques. One option is for the team first to discuss each principle and gain a full understanding of what each one means. If the team is using an external facilitator then he or she can provide examples from other organizations of how these principles have been applied in other settings. The next step is to write the principles on a piece of flip chart paper and post this on a wall in the room where everyone can see it or put them on an acetate that can be projected on to a screen. The third step involves the team brainstorming all the ways it can apply these principles to the process under review. The team should be reminded of the rules of brainstorming, which state there should be no criticism of any idea, that the team should aim for quantity not quality at this stage, there should be freewheeling rather than constrained, analytical ideas, every idea should be recorded and the team should 'incubate' these ideas to develop them to their fullest potential rather than evaluate them immediately.

The team should aim to fill at least four of five pages of flip chart paper with their ideas, which equates to about two hundred ideas. During the brainstorming session the facilitator should ensure that the team concentrates on all of the principles equally, and generates several ideas for the application of each one. At this stage it does not matter if these ideas overlap, or even conflict with each other. An alternative procedure that we have used to similar effect involves writing each principle on the top of a separate piece of flip chart paper. The team considers each principle in turn and fills the remainder of the page with ideas about how that particular principle can be applied to the process being re-engineered.

Whatever procedure the team uses, the main purpose of the session is for the team to generate alternative ways of meeting the requirements of the customers of the process and not to be constrained by the assumptions that govern how work is performed in the organization. The team needs to think 'out of the box' and seek ideas that mirror the solutions to the nine-dot problem in terms of creativity and their ability to break out of current ways of thinking about work. It is helpful to have on display a statement of the process vision so that the team is reminded of what it wants to achieve from the process, and a list of process enablers, on view as a way of generating ideas about how they can be put to use.

After the brainstorming session, which should take about half an hour, the team should take a short break to refresh their minds, and then return to the list of ideas generated and quickly scan them. Sometimes it helps to have a second, five-minute brainstorming session after this break. We have found that often the most creative ideas are generated during this session. Alternatively, individuals may simply add any ideas that occur to them following their scan of the entire list.

The meeting should be brought to a close and the members of the team left to incubate the ideas that have been suggested. Over the course of the next few days some of these ideas will flower into suggestions that are capable of meeting the process vision and achieving all the performance targets that have been set for it. The task for the re-engineering team is nurture these ideas and to develop the process enablers that will allow them to be put into practice. It should use the process mapping techniques outlined in Chapter 8 to do this, thus representing the new process visually on paper.

The period of development will take several weeks, and the team may have to alter its original design to take account of factors not originally considered or to develop even further some of the possibilities hinted at during the early stages of re-engineering.

PROCESS IMPROVEMENT TECHNIQUES

Although the new process is likely to be very different from the one it is replacing if it is to meet the challenging targets articulated in the process vision, parts of it will remain the same. Thus although several sub-processes may be omitted, combined with others, outsourced to suppliers or handed to customers to perform, others may remain. The sub-processes will be represented by the same circles in both old and new process maps (data flow diagrams). This does not mean, however, that the team should simply preserve the *status quo*. The changes elsewhere in the process provide a perfect opportunity to re-visit sub-processes that remain from the old version and subject them to a rigorous analysis of improvement possibilities. Several tried and tested techniques are available to help highlight where and how changes should be made. These changes will not be on the scale of the re-engineering work the team has recently performed on the main part of the process, and the aim is to improve and streamline a sub-process which has already been deemed to be worth saving from the original. A flow chart of the sub-process is most useful in achieving these improvements, and there are four principal ways in which the team can concentrate its efforts on steamlining the process it represents.

FIVE QUESTION ANALYSIS

As the name suggests, five question analysis involves asking five questions of each step of the process represented in the flow chart:

- What is the purpose?
- Where is it performed?
- When is it performed?
- Who performs it?
- How is it performed?

The aim is not simply to answer each question but to generate alternative answers. For example, in questioning the purpose of the step the team should consider what else would achieve that same purpose, as well as considering whether the step had a useful purpose at all. Similarly, when discussing where the step is performed, the team should ask itself whether that step could usefully be performed elsewhere, reducing delays and transport costs.

The team should not be constrained by limited definitions of the precise meaning of the question. Each is open to different interpretations and this should be seen as a strength of the technique in as much as it can generate different ways of looking at the process. In this way, in asking 'when' the step is performed and whether it could be carried out at some other time, the team should consider this question of timing in relation to as many events as possible. Alternative answers might be: 'before a mistake has occurred', 'before a customer has complained', 'after we have checked for errors', 'before we start', and so on.

Although this is not a complex analysis, it is remarkably effective and we have used it to achieve small but significant improvements in all manner of work processes. In Chapter 8 we mentioned a team of hospital porters who flow-charted the process of getting patients from wards to the operating theatres, and returning them after surgery. The flow chart showed that the first action performed by a porter upon arriving at the ward was to check whether the patient was there and was ready to be taken to the theatre. In working through the five question analysis the team first considered the purpose of this step and agreed that it was valid; they then questioned whether it could be performed elsewhere and at a different time. This immediately prompted the suggestion that the best time to check would be before the porter set off on his journey to the ward, as this would save an unnecessary journey if the patient had in the meantime been transferred to another ward. If the porter telephoned the ward before setting off, not only could he check whether the patient was there and avoid a possible unnecessary journey, he could also alert the ward staff to his pending arrival and this would enable them to get the patient ready for theatre before he arrived. The flow chart showed that after checking the patient was in fact on the ward, there was a delay while the ward staff prepared the patient for theatre. So by moving the patient check to a much earlier point in the process (before the porter leaves the theatre) the team was able to reduce the number of unnecessary journeys to wards that no longer housed the patient, reduce the number of cancelled operations due to not being able to locate a patient that had been transferred to another ward and reduce the delays incurred by porters while they waited for patients to be prepared for surgery.

VALUE ADDED ANALYSIS

An additional technique is to perform a value added analysis on a process that has been flow-charted. This simple yet effective analysis highlights steps in a process that may be unnecessary, since they add no real value. All too often, steps are added to a process because the process has been poorly designed in the first place, and exist only to cope with the difficulties this poor design causes. For example, steps that involve transporting goods or items are often necessary only because something is produced in the wrong place. If the item was produced where it was needed, transportation would not be necessary, thus reducing delays due to transportation.

To conduct a value added analysis the team needs to classify each step in a process according to one of the following categories:

- adds real value
- adds business value
- adds no value

Steps that add value are those that actually make a difference to the final output of a process and which directly contribute to meeting the customer's requirements. This would include steps in the physical production of a product to customer specifications, or in the case of a service it could include the addition of any information required by the customer or the actual provision of that service itself. To return to the team of hospital porters, their flow chart showed the process of getting patients to and from wards consisted of more than 30 steps, yet there were just three steps that actually added value: anaesthetize the patient, operate on the patient, recover the patient. We can imagine how the patient would feel if any of these were omitted! Although other steps were important, they were not intrinsically necessary and reflected the design of the process rather than its fundamental purpose.

Steps that add business value are those that are required by the organization but which add no value from the customer's point of view. They include, for example, recording information that is used by other departments, ordering materials and preparing reports. Sometimes activities appear to add business value because we believe they produce outputs that are required by someone else, yet further investigation often reveals they have no purpose at all. A manager once told us how a sales team in his company would every month produce very detailed accounts of their off-sales activities. When he asked them why they had to produce such detailed accounts the sales team replied that the information was needed by the central office, although they had little idea why or how the information was used. Further enquiries at the central office showed that no one there knew why the salespeople produced the figures they received once a month, but everyone assumed that the figures must be important to the salespeople since why else would they go to so much trouble! More detailed investigation revealed that four years earlier a management trainee had requested the figures be collected for two months for a survey he was conducting. He had long since moved on in the company, but each month the figures were collected with no one remembering or even questioning why.

Activities like this can be found in every organization. Tasks are performed even though the original reason has long since disappeared, and at first sight they appear to be fulfilling a need, although always for someone else in some other department. In identifying these tasks as adding business value a team should be certain that business value is added and that there is a genuine customer.

Finally, tasks that add no value either to the customer or to the business are non-value-adding tasks. These include rework, the storage of files, materials or equipment in the anticipation that it may one day be needed by someone, the collection of information that is not used for any explicit purpose, chasing up on the progress of a job, correcting errors and mistakes, authorizing requests, and so on. Such activities may exist because of poor process design that results in unnecessary errors, transportation, storage or delays. Or they may exist as relics of once useful activities, like those described above.

Using a flow chart to identify all the steps in a process, a value added analysis involves categorizing each one as either value added, business value added, or non-value added. A text highlighter is useful here, and allows a visual assessment of the proportion of steps in the process accounted by each of these categories. The next task is to consider whether any of the value added steps can be optimized, perhaps by performing them quicker or at a lower cost. Can some of the business value added steps be eliminated or their cost minimized? And finally, how can the non-value added steps be eliminated by improving process design (using the five question analysis), removing the causes of some problems, and empowering people to make decisions where previously they had to seek authorization?

People are often astonished at the very low number of value added steps that exist in a process, and this is a very useful technique to highlight that fact and concentrate efforts on maximizing these and reducing other steps.

BUREAUCRACY ELIMINATION

Bureaucracy elimination is similar to a value added analysis, since bureaucratic procedures are those that add no value to the organization or the customer, yet continue to exist and grow due to a range of seemingly unstoppable factors. The main difference is that in conducting this type of analysis, a team is looking at a specific type of activity. Typically, bureaucratic steps in a process are those that involve checking, authorizing, storing, recording, producing multiple copies and approving. They exist largely because of psychological factors, such as a failure to trust individuals, fear of blame for errors, the need to justify one's role in the organization, a lack of self-worth or pleasure at detecting errors made by others. There is no simple formula for identifying and eliminating bureaucracy, other than questioning the need and value of having them and how the process can still be effective without them.

CYCLE TIME ANALYSIS

Cycle time analysis also uses a flow chart, but does so by showing the time it takes for the process to complete a full cycle. Starting with the first step in the process, a cumulative time index is drawn on to the chart, showing the time elapsed until the process is completed. The time taken to perform each step (referred to as process time) should also be recorded. Once they have done this, a team can compare the full process time as a proportion of the elapsed time of the process. It is not unusual to find ratios of around 5–10 per cent. In other words, only about 10 per cent of the time taken to perform a process is actually spent doing something. The rest of the time is taken up with delays, dead time while an item rests in a person's in-tray and transportation.

There are several ways in which the entire cycle time can be reduced while maintaining process time and thereby improving this ratio. Some tasks may be carried out in parallel with others where previously they were performed serially. The flow chart will also show whether products or items flow back and forth between departments and, if this is the case, it may be possible to combine all the steps carried out in one location to one point in time, so reducing transportation delays. By better co-ordinating activities it is also possible to reduce the amount of time documents are left waiting in in-trays for collection. For example, if weekly time sheets are collected at 10.00 a.m. on a Friday morning it makes sense to ensure that all are present and completed by 5.00 p.m. on Thursday evening. Changing the location at which goods are produced can also reduce time spent in transportation. In sum, there are many ways in which the time between activities in a process can be reduced through careful planning and design.

These four methods demonstrate the variety of ways in which processes can be streamlined to operate more quickly, with lower costs and with fewer errors. They represent the traditional approach to process improvement, since the basic assumptions on which the process is based is not really challenged and no attempt is made to replace the process with something entirely different. On their own they can result in significant improvements in process time and performance, but they cannot achieve the step changes in performance that the techniques of re-engineering are capable of achieving. However, rather than discard them in favour of the latter, the re-engineering team should ideally use a dual approach, where streamlining is performed on all sub-processes within the new process. In this way they can achieve the best of both worlds.

11 Managing the Change

Many people make the mistake of thinking that managing the change is simply a matter of introducing a new, usually computer, system. This is far from the truth because the actual BPR project will have defined the new system in detail, and the team should have thought through the best approach in a technical sense. This would include, for example, whether or not any prototyping was necessary, the logical phases, timing and so on.

In this chapter we do not focus on these aspects, rather, using our experience in managing the introduction of radically re-engineered processes, we consider issues concerning the organization as a whole, the teams in the re-engineered areas and the individuals who will be doing the work. These are aspects that are central to success and yet are commonly forgotten or treated as trivial afterthoughts. They are not.

At the organizational level the first issue that should be considered is the compatibility of the human effects of the re-engineering process with the organization's philosophy of working or values. Many organizations have statements that define their underlying values, and many of these include the subject of their employees, for example 'our employees represent our most valuable resource'. In some cases these statements are well considered and well meaning, in others they represent not much more than platitudes.

It is possible, if not likely, that the results of the re-engineering will appear to be in conflict with the stated philosophy, which is arguably the most important 'glue' within the culture of the organization. If this is the case, it must not be left un-addressed since this will inevitably damage both the organization's philosophy and peoples' attitude to BPR.

The question of course is how to deal with any conflicts, either real or apparent, that exist between the philosophy and the results of BPR. In either event the senior team needs to meet and to work through the issue in a very thorough manner. The ever-present danger in the process of doing this is that those involved will simply rationalize the situation, their decisions and their behaviour, which is why it usually will be help-

145

ful to have a skilled external facilitator attend the event explicitly to ensure that this does not happen.

The conclusion of the discussion is usually either:

1. there is a clear potential 'violation' of the philosophy that needs to be addressed within the spirit of the statement, in other words without changing the philosophy, or
2. there is a 'violation' but the organization realizes that the stated philosophy was a platitude which it is not interested in supporting, or
3. there is no 'violation'.

In the last case there may or may not still be a need for explanation to the workforce; it is certainly dangerous to assume that the explanation is obvious.

In the first situation the outcomes of the re-engineering project need to be considered in the context of the philosophy statement. This result can normally be achieved without losing the benefits of BPR, but may slow the rate at which they are forthcoming. Handled properly in terms of communication with staff this process can significantly help people's belief in the philosophy and the credibility of the entire change process that it and indeed BPR are a part of.

The second situation is one we have little sympathy with but, unfortunately, it occurs frequently. The options are to abandon the philosophy either implicitly or explicitly and possibly come back to a redefinition at some point in the future when people may have forgotten it, or to abandon the whole of the change process of which the philosophy was a part and to concentrate solely on the short-term gains that can come out of BPR. Any of these options is clearly an unsatisfactory state of affairs which demonstrates yet again that decisions about such things as organizational philosophy should not be taken lightly.

The third possibility is that there is no incompatibility between the outcomes of the BPR project and the philosophy of the organization. As has already been said, this will need stating clearly and explicitly and should be seen as a good opportunity for some internal marketing of the whole process of change and development, and the philosophy and BPR as parts of this.

The next important aspect of managing this kind of change at the organizational level concerns trust. In most organizations this is a commodity in short supply; a situation that inevitably damages performance and, since BPR involves getting the best out of those who work with the process with the minimum of extraneous management, this represents another issue that cannot be ignored.

From the outset the term 'BPR' is likely to evoke considerable anxiety and also a set of assumptions about what might or 'will' happen as a result of it. The assumptions and anxiety are a consequence of BPR's reputation which will of course be exaggerated and put into a negative light by the 'scaremongers' in the organization. A compensating strategy is required to prevent this happening because negative news travels faster, is more interesting to most people and is more readily believed than positive news.

If there is a need to develop a high-trust environment, which there is for any organization that wishes to be successful over the long term, a policy of open communication between people at all levels should be promoted. The purpose of a high-trust environment, from the organization's point of view, is to prove to people that they are hearing all of the relevant news, not just what the organization wants them to hear. Such a policy will take time to demonstrate conclusively and progress will have to be well 'marketed' internally.

The dual principles that underpin the development of a trusting and open relationship between different people and different levels of the organization are first, not to live lies since they will always be found out in the end, and second, that for most people bad news is better than no news.

The next element concerns the organization's mission and the need for readjustment as part of managing the change occasioned by the BPR project. The use of BPR will, by its very nature, always be high profile and there is a danger that some people forget just what the fundamental purpose of the organization is and, secondly, that BPR is a means of helping to achieve it rather than something that has been introduced simply because 'it seemed like a good idea at the time'. Therefore, a part of the process of implementing the results of the project should always be to explain to people in the organization how BPR helps with the achievement of the mission.

Leadership is the next ingredient in managing the change. Of course this is obvious but it does need both to be said and provided, which is often the difficult part. It should also be mentioned that the bigger the change the more leadership is likely to be required and that because of its radical nature the results of a BPR project are likely to be seen as big in the eyes of those in the organization concerned. The main elements of the leadership that is needed are those that have been mentioned already in this chapter, a reinforcement of the underlying philosophy of the organization and its mission, including how the use of BPR has and will help and, importantly, a feedback and communication process that develops high levels of trust and confidence that the organization and those in it are in good hands.

Finally at the organization level there is a need for a clear and well-considered internal marketing strategy that supports the implementation process. This is an aspect that organizations often either forget or handle very poorly, and yet it is such an important element because it deals with the overall perception that people will have and this will influence behaviour for good or ill.

The next level at which the process of implementation needs to be managed is that of the work group, specifically the group or groups that represent the newly re-engineered process. Of course jobs will have changed, quite possibly to a point that they are unrecognizable when compared to the originals. Because of this 'technical' training is likely to be needed, but BPR is also about developing more effective teamwork, high levels of empowerment and a recognition among the work groups that they have responsibility for the ongoing improvement of their part of the overall process. This aspect must not be underestimated since it is key to achieving the best possible results from the project both immediately and in its aftermath.

Training and support in the skills of team working and the techniques of improvement will have to be provided, and often a change in leadership style on the part of the leaders of the newly formed work teams is needed. Most organizations, before they commence re-engineering, are structured traditionally as functional hierarchies managed in a fairly directive fashion, and most see nothing wrong in this neither do they perceive much alternative.

Classically the role of management in a functional hierachy is to control and police the operation, and is seen as being necessary because the underlying belief of the approach is that people are not really to be trusted. If the 'shop floor' is not to be trusted, it is a small step to say that supervisors who are the 'controller/ cops' should themselves be subject to policing. So, over time, the situation in many organizations has become one where there are layers upon layers of people doing progressively more senior jobs that are controlling and policing the level below.

BPR is sometimes seen by people as a way of eliminating the need for people to do jobs by utilizing new technology more effectively. In fact it also obviates the need for a range of traditional management roles because an underlying assumption is that if provided with the right conditions, training and support, people will be motivated and able to perform their work without the need for layers of management to control and police them.

If BPR is introduced properly as a part of an overall change and development process, the role of the team leader becomes just that, the leader of the team. The requirement in this role is for coaching and counselling rather than controlling and policing and so it is imperative that people in these roles are given the appropriate training, back-up and support as they work on developing and then using these new skills.

As far as the work group is concerned there is the issue of sense of direction or the clarity that exists concerning the re-engineered process and the achievement of the organization's fundamental purpose. It goes without saying that if the members of the work group do not see or understand how the new process should contribute to the quest towards the mission of the organization as a whole and their own part of it, it is unlikely that their work will optimize the potential gains. Therefore, the team leader needs to be sure that sufficient clarification is given on this subject, including the opportunity for exploration and discussion of different views, and that enough reinforcement is also provided, especially in the early days.

The individuals involved in the change should be managed with an appropriate degree of sensitivity, skill and care. In fact this is often the area that is least well considered and executed in many organizations because only one of the important dimensions is dealt with at all. Two categories of individual need to be considered, those who have a part to play after re-engineering and those who do not.

Most organizations, and all that have any sense, recognize that the way redundant employees are treated both actually and in peoples' perception, is an issue of significance. This is the case regardless of whether redundancy is being handled voluntarily, by attrition or through a compulsory programme. BPR, implemented well, achieves massive benefits for the organization and so for the most part there is usually the opportunity for the organization to be generous in the severance package that it designs, not only in the direct financial sense but also through job search support, retirement planning and training and so on.

Organizations often structure generous severance packages but forget to sell and market them within the organization, and sometimes outside. Selling and marketing will always be a necessary part of managing change since there is always a negative element who may gain attention and support quite out of proportion to their numbers if their negativity is allowed to go apparently without question.

So most organizations try at least to offer reasonably generous and sometimes extremely advantageous arrangements to those who will no longer be required. The remarkable omission when it comes to handling individuals through this process of traumatic change is that in most organizations no attention at all is paid to the needs of those who stay, despite the fact that it is nearly always them that 'suffer' most through the whole process. It is almost as if the organization is assuming that these people either will, or should be, so grateful for having been given the opportunity to stay that they require no further thought or attention.

If such is the organization's view, it is a dangerous and incorrect assumption since most people that stay do suffer more than those that leave under whatever circumstances. Some of the negative consequences that so often occur in the implementation of change of this kind can be traced directly to a failure to manage those that stay in an appropriate and sensitive enough way.

Many of the individuals who stay go through a number of recognizable phases in their reaction to the new situation. The first symptom that so often comes to the fore is guilt. This can reveal itself in a number of ways, for example with people saying things like, 'what right have I got still to be here when Fred and Sally are not?'

The second response is often fear, occasioned by the dawning of a belief that what has already happened cannot possibly be the end of the story; that there are bound to be more phases and that, since 'I' have no right to be here now, it is inevitable that my name will be at the top of the list of those to go the next time round.

The third symptom is anger which is where the attention is turned on to the organization itself. Typically at this stage the person is saying things like, 'what right do "they" have to turn people like Fred and Sally out on to the streets. They gave them the best ten years of their life and what good did it do them. "They" are very good at talking about the need for company loyalty now just look at what kind of loyalty "they" have to us, it's disgusting and I wish I had gone.'

Finally there is the stage of defence, which is where the employee begins to feel very vulnerable, for example, 'All the outside jobs in the area will have been taken by those who have already left. They were always better than me really, so I stand no chance without moving away from the area, and I can't possibly do that, all my friends are here. My best bet is to keep my head down. I am very worried about my family and our security.'

The damage that is done by allowing these sorts of beliefs to develop and fester can be very serious, which makes it all the more surprising that so few organizations have any understanding of what is happening, let alone any coherent strategy and plan for dealing with the situation. To understand and be able to deal with this we need an understanding of attitudes, what they are and how they change and can be influenced to change.

For a word so often used, and with such passion, there seems to be little understanding of its meaning and still less about the process by which they change. Yet the subject of attitudes is among the most thoroughly researched in the field of social psychology. We certainly know more about it than we do about most other aspects in this field.

An attitude can best be defined as 'a predisposition to act', and any attitude about anything contains two distinct parts. The first is everything that we know about a particular subject, our database if you like. This is the cognitive element and for ease of understanding here could be said to include our beliefs which, however irrational they might be, still form an important part of what we claim to know about the subject. The second part concerns our feelings about the issue, the affective element. So our attitudes reflect both our hearts and our heads.

The next relevant point is that human beings have an urge to keep the different parts of any particular attitude in balance because it is psychologically very uncomfortable to be in a situation where our head is telling us one thing and our heart is saying something different. Every human being will act to reduce this 'dissonance' and to bring the attitude in question back into balance. In the normal course of events when our attitude to something is in balance we will not change it since we do not willingly tend to create the sort of discomfort that is involved in disrupting our personal *status quo*.

This balance is very relevant to the whole issue of managing the individual consequences of BPR projects. If we assume that before the advent of BPR people's attitude to the organization was in balance, which is likely, and if we take the charitable view that it was positive, the result of the BPR project is probably to have disrupted this balance among the individuals that remain for all the reasons that have already been described. Therefore it is possible (if not likely) that the previously positive attitude could also have been transformed into a negative one. The challenge in managing the change is to convert this back into a positive one, since otherwise the benefits of the BPR project will not be optimized. Quite simply the people involved will not have the motivation or the overall positive spirit to make it work.

So the question is how to help people to change their attitude to the organization now that they both 'know' and 'feel' that the organization has behaved in a way that leads them to this negative view. Leon Festinger provides us with the most useful and usable theory of attitude change. His Theory of Cognitive Dissonance states that: 'If people are induced to say or to do something that is contrary to their private attitude [thoughts and feelings], they will tend to modify their thoughts and feelings [attitude] to bring them in line with their new behaviour.' He adds an important rider, however, which is that the greater the pressure used to bring about the change in behaviour (beyond the minimum needed to achieve it) the less the attitude will change.[1]

Festinger explains this process as one of rationalization. We all need to be able to justify our behaviour to ourselves and we spend much of our time doing just that either to others or simply within our own minds. A typical reaction might be as follows, 'so, this organization that I have worked for over the last number of years engaged in a BPR project as a result of which "the world has been turned upside down" and many people, including some of my friends, were declared redundant. I used to think that this organization, of which I am part, cared for people, but it is clear to me now that this was a sham. When they did this my first reaction was one of shock, I felt let down, almost betrayed. Now, as I think about it, the organization underneath it all was like this all the time; I remember when they...'.

In this example the person's feelings have changed and to justify this he or she has added to their knowledge-base examples of 'facts' that fit with the new feelings. The result is a changed attitude that is in balance and which will remain until and unless something happens to disrupt the balance again. This is precisely the process that happens with many people when faced with changes to the *status quo* of the magnitude occasioned by BPR projects, and unless managed with skill and care the consequences, clearly, can be very damaging.

So the first step in managing the change at the individual level is to diagnose any changes in attitude that are apparent among people, notably changes from positive to negative. Sometimes these will be obvious, but on other occasions they may need 'teasing out' since some will hide their true feelings from the management but be vociferous in private discussions with colleagues.

The second step is to try to understand the basis of the attitude shift since this will give valuable clues in how to address it. For example, was the dissonance caused by a shift in feelings or was it more influenced by the new 'facts'. The purpose here is not to criticize or to defend, it is to understand because it will be much more difficult to help someone to shift their attitude if we do not understand 'where they are coming from'. People can only start from where they are at the moment.

The third step is to develop a plan to help the person address the change that has happened and, hopefully, to turn the attitude into a positive one. The first problem is which aspect of attitude to concentrate on, knowledge or feelings, or whether some combination of the two is the most appropriate approach. The idea here is to decide how best to try and help the person disrupt the balance of their attitude; sometimes it will be easiest to change the knowledge-base and in other situations working on the person's feelings will be better.

Once this decision has been made it is a matter of arranging the best way of handling the interaction. This will vary from situation to situation and could involve anything from going to the pub socially with the person concerned to arranging a formal meeting to discuss the underlying rationale for using BPR in this particular organization. More than one meeting may be required.

As far as who should facilitate this process is concerned, ideally the person's manager should do the job, but only if he or she has the knowledge and skill required. In our experience this is a good opportunity to help in the development of more appropriate coaching and facilitative styles of management, and as a part of the implementation of the BPR project it is our strongly held view that all the managers who are in any way related to the project should be trained as facilitators. Ultimately so too should all of the other managers.

The successful implementation of BPR projects requires much more than merely introducing the technical aspects of the solution. As can be seen there are a wide range of issues that need to be taken into account at the levels of the organization, the work teams and also the individuals who play such a key role in the success of the new process.

BPR is exciting. It offers the chance for quantum leaps in performance. It is subject to the same dangers as other techniques, but these dangers are for the most part known and understood, and have been covered in this book. Careful use of the methodology that has been explained and skilled management of the process aspects of such projects should ensure that any organization can use the technique, gain the benefits and so help to assure their survival and success in the future. But never forget that we live in a changing world; to paraphrase Winston Churchill, 'BPR is not an end, it is not even the beginning of the end, but it might be the end of the beginning.'

NOTES

1. Festinger, L. (1957), *A Theory of Cognitive Dissonance*, Stanford: Stanford University Press.

Further Reading

GROUPS AND GROUP PROBLEM-SOLVING

Management Teams, Why They Succeed or Fail by R. Meredith Belbin (Oxford: Heinemann, 1981).
This is Belbin's main book on the subject of team roles. It includes a detailed explanation of the different roles, and material describing unsuccessful and successful teams. It also contains a self-perception inventory.
Decision Making in Small Groups by Albert Kowitz and Thomas Knutson (Boston, Mass.: Allyn and Bacon, 1980).
This is a technical book which includes sections on the structure of interactions, groups and decisions. It also analyses group process problems. It is useful if you are interested in studying groups, but is not easy to read.
Group Dynamics by Marvin Shaw (New York: McGraw Hill, 1971).
This is a technical book which is not easy to read, but it deals with some of the basics of group dynamics, for example group size, seating and other special arrangements, the social structure of groups, the task environment and different types of group.
Problem Solving in Groups by Mike Robson (Aldershot: Gower, 1993).
This book is a practical guide to solving problems in groups. It contains a step-by-step problem-solving process and includes the detail of how to use the different techniques successfully. Some of the techniques that are included are well-known, others are new.

INDIVIDUAL BEHAVIOUR

I'm OK – You're OK by Thomas Harris (London: Pan, 1970).
This is the seminal work on life positions. The book contains material on transactional analysis, which was the basis of Harris's ideas on life positions, and so it is useful in that it covers both subjects in sufficient depth. It is also easy to read and digest.

ORGANIZATION CHANGE AND DEVELOPMENT

The Journey to Excellence by Mike Robson (Wantage: MRA International, 1986).
This contains a coherent model for the development of organizations and the achievement of sustained excellence. It incorporates the principles and practice of Total Quality.
Organisation Development by Warner Burke (Reading, Mass.: Addison Wesley, 1987).
This provides an overview of the field of Organization Development (OD), and includes a definition, the models of change that OD has been based on historically, and chapters on the process and management of change.
Process Consultation (vols 1 and 2) by Edgar Schein (Reading, Mass.: Addison Wesley, 1987 and 1988).
These books describe 'process consultation' and the alternative styles of consultancy. They include much useful advice for the internal or external consultant who wishes to learn about and develop a capability in process consultancy.

PROCESS MANAGEMENT

Re-engineering the Corporation: A Manifesto for Business Revolution by Michael Hammer and James Champy (London: Nicholas Brealey Publishing, 1993).
This provides a useful background to Business Process Re-engineering, although the case studies that take up the last third of the book add little. A good introduction to the topic but with little practical advice.
Process Innovation by Thomas Davenport (Boston, Mass.: Harvard Business School Press, 1993).
A largely academic textbook on Business Process Re-engineering with some useful guidelines and plenty of detailed references to other texts and articles. This is definitely for the serious-minded reader who wants to research BPR in depth.
Business Process Improvement by James Harrington (New York: McGraw-Hill, 1991).
Written before the advent of BPR, this book gives a good account of process management and the various techniques for process improvement.

Index

accounting systems 41
adaptability 46
anger 150
anxiety 29, 42, 44, 147 *see also* fear
appraisal systems 118
assumptions, questioning 4, 5, 14, 75, 109, 138
attitudes, worker 150–52 *see also* employee relations
authorization 13, 14, 113, 125–126, 143
automation 110 *see also* technology
Automated Call Distributor (ACD) 129
autonomous work teams 114–15

bar codes 137
Belbin, M.J. 56
benchmarking current processes 82–3
better service 6
brainstorming 23, 58, 64, 80, 81, 84, 138
bureaucracy 11–12, 70, 113, 143
    elimination 113, 143
Business Process Management 2, 13
Business Process Re-engineering (BPR) ix, 1, 2–7, 18, 27–36
    applying 138–9
    benefits 28, 39, 41, 91
    books on 27, 28, 33, 155–6
    definition 4–6
    in-house executive briefing 27–8, 58
    managing 6–8 *see also* process management
    methodology 19–22
    origins 2–3
    problems 32
    project stages 33–6
    resources needed 34–5, 57–9
    savings 32
    success rates 33
    time necessary 35–6
    understanding 67–77
    workshops 27, 34, 58, 62, 63, 64, 65, 82

business processes 11–13 *see also* process
    definition 15, 19–20
business strategy 69–70, 83–4

career planning 116–17
'caring' organizations 30
case teams 115, 116
change
    managing 43–4, 145–53
    processes 8
    view of 8, 43–4
chief executives 22, 24
communication 12–13, 40, 41, 137, 146, 147
    centralizing 137
computers 110–13 *see also* information technology
consultants 34–5, 52–4
    dangers of 53
    expert 52, 53
    external 52–4, 58
    process 52, 53
continuous improvement 35–6
co-ordinator 54–5
    selection 55
core processes 17
cost effectiveness 6
creativity 5, 23, 34, 80, 105–9, 122–3, 138
critical success factors (CSFs) 64, 65, 68, 69, 70
customer
    awareness 18, 25
    expectations 70, 72
    external 70, 127–8
    internal 70, 78
    participation 127–32
    primary 15, 16, 47, 78
    recognition 69
    requirements 78–80, 84
    secondary 78
cycle time analysis 143-4

157

INDEX

data flow
  diagrams 88, 91–4, 102, 123, 136–7, 139
  levelling 94
databases, shared 137
Davenport, T.H. 2
decentralization 137
decision analysis systems 113
decision-making 14, 114, 115
  consensus 63
defensiveness 150
Delphi (modified) 58
de-mediation 111
destructive competition 12
Drucker, P. 2

effectiveness 2, 19, 45, 46, 80
efficiency 2, 11, 21, 45, 46, 80
Electronic Data Interchange (EDI) 111, 129, 130, 137
e-mail 112, 137
employee
  morale 40 *see also* fear, anxiety
  recognition 44
  relations 28, 31, 40–3, 145, 146, 147, 148, 149–50
enthusiasm 44, 49
executive briefing, in-house 27–8, 58
expert systems 112, 127
external assessment 29

facilitators 23, 35, 48, 50–2, 53, 57, 58, 63, 68, 80, 99, 109, 138, 146, 153
  selection 52
  training 58
Fayol, H. 11
fear 3, 31, 40, 41, 42, 43, 44, 49, 150
Festinger, L. 151
fishbone diagrams 58
Five Question Analysis 140–41
flexibility in workforce 115
flow charts 75, 87, 97–102, 103, 142, 144
  problems 87
force field analysis 58
Ford, H. 114
functional management 12–13, 28, 148
functional specialization 11, 12
  problems 12–13, 14, 18, 19, 25

generalism 122

Hammer, M. 2
human effects of re-engineering 145
  see also redundancy, job security, attitudes (worker)
human resource enablers 113–19

In-Department Evaluation of Activity (IDEA) 2, 40
information technology (IT) 6, 58–9, 110–13
initiatives (BPR)
  other 38–40
  starting 29
input/output consistency 96–7
input reduction 135–7
internal marketing strategy 147, 148

job security 31–2, 40–3, 149–50

key processes, defining 61, 65, 81–2
key success factors 23–4

leadership 147, 148
Local Area Network (LAN) installation 132–5
lifetime employment 115–16
logical levelling 79, 84

management 6, 11–25, 145–53
  development 118–19
Mayo, E. 114
Method for Analysing Processes (MAP) 2
mission statements 8, 22, 63, 64, 86, 145, 146, 147 *see also* vision
motivation, worker 6, 114 *see also* attitudes (worker)

network links 112–13
Neuro-Lingustic Programming 79, 85

organization
  assessment 23–4, 29
  'caring' 25–6
  development 5–6, 118–19
  structure 21–5, 39
organizational and management development 118–19
outputs, primary and secondary 15–17
ownership, importance of 45–7

'people' issues 30–2
performance management 106–7
problem-solving activities 5, 19, 35, 109, 138
  cross-functional 18–19
process, administrative 66
process boundaries 15–18, 66, 73, 76–8
  defining 68–9
process change, managing 145–53
process consultancy 52–3
process, cross-functional 66, 69, 91
process description/definition 68, 76–7

process design 109–31
process dictionary 95–6
process enablers 109–19, 137
process environment diagrams 88–91, 94
process improvement techniques 139–44
process management 2, 5, 11–25, 145–53
   benefits 18
   defining 19–21
   in practice 18–25
process mapping 87–103, 136–7
process obsolescence 1–2
process, operational 66
process owner 20–1, 35, 45–8
   selection 47–8
Process Perception Analysis (PPA) 2
Process Quality Management (PQM) 2, 19, 20, 34, 62, 63, 68
   workshop 62, 63, 64, 65, 69
process rating 69, 80–82
process selection 34, 69
process structures 21–5
process, support 66
process, understanding 75–86
process, vision of new 82–6, 139
processes, multiple versions of 134–5
project duration 30–1

Quality Circles 40

rationalization 151
reconciliation 135–6
redeployment 31, 32, 41, 42
redundancy 31–2, 40–43, 149
resources 30, 57–9
responsibility, cross-functional 46–7
Robson, M. 2

savings 32
Scientific Management 11
senior management 35, 37–8
Short, J.E. 2
six-word diagram 58
specialization 122
starting initiatives 33–4
Statistical Process Control 40

status quo 1, 44, 47, 79, 132, 139, 151, 152
steering groups 28, 34, 35
Structured Process Analysis (SPA) 87–103
   guidelines for using 94–102
   maximizing use of 91–4
sub-optimal structures 22
suppliers, external 130, 132–33
support processes 17

Tavistock Institute of Human Relations 119
Taylor, F.W. 11, 114
team leader 35, 48–50, 58, 148
   selection 49–50
   training 53
team 61
   members 35, 38, 55–7, 58
   process-oriented 118
   recognition 44
   size 122–6
technology 5, 6, 58 *see also* information technology
Theory of Cognitive Dissonance 151
threats 3, 8, 25
360° appraisals 118
tools 105–119
Total Quality Management (TQM) ix, 2, 6, 7, 13, 28, 40, 127, 130
tracking 111
training 35, 41, 44, 58, 148
   facilitation 46, 47, 58
trust (high trust environment) 146, 147

Value Added Analysis 141–3
vision of new process 3, 82–6, 129, 139
   statement 84–5 *see also* mission statements

Weber, M. 11
Wilson, H. 1
workforce *see* employee relations, redundancy, fear, anxiety

Young, E. 33